PR(The)OMISE

Make Your

Life Rich

by Discovering

Your Best Self

Victor Davich

ST. MARTIN'S GRIFFIN ⚹ New York

Neither the publisher nor the author is engaged in
rendering professional advice or services to the
individual reader. The ideas, procedures, and suggestions
contained in this book are not intended as
a substitute for consulting with your physician.
Neither the author nor the publisher shall be liable
or responsible for any loss or damage allegedly arising from
any information or suggestion in this book.

www.stmartins.com

Book design by Patrice Sheridan

LIBRARY OF CONGRESS CATALOGING-IN-PUBLICATION DATA

Davich, Victor N., 1952–
    The promise : make your life rich by discovering your best self / Victor
Davich.—1st ed.
        p.   cm.
    ISBN-13: 978-0-312-37815-8
    ISBN-10: 0-312-37815-7
    1. Self-actualization (Psychology)   I. Title.
    BF637.S4D368   2008
    158.1—dc22

                                                    2008025086

First Edition: December 2008

10 9 8 7 6 5 4 3 2 1

Contents

Stop!

Take a deep breath. Close your eyes. And think about this: What do you want most in life? What is the treasure that will make you happy beyond even your wildest dreams? That can never be taken away from you?

Now imagine a marvelous chest that contains this treasure. It's been waiting for you all this time to be opened. Imagine it as vividly as possible. Because guess what? *You're sitting on top of it—at this very moment.*

Do you think this impossible? Even crazy? Or are you open to looking? If so, this book will empower you to reclaim your treasure: the Promise of your birthright, the immeasurable riches that lie within you and always have.

Don't be angry at yourself for not seeing your treasure sooner. It's not how long you've forgotten where it is. It's how soon you remember.

Don't waste another moment. Begin now. Just turn the page. . . .

Welcome to The Promise

The Promise is your absolute entitlement to be Your Best Self: who you truly are, not *who you mistakenly think you are;* that person people would scorn, shun, and spurn if they "knew the real me."

You might be rolling your eyes, saying to yourself, "Right, I've heard this one before. What's going to be different this time?" My answer is simply this: The Promise has already been kept. It's waiting for you to accept it.

If this is true, you might be thinking, "Well, if so, who needs you and your book?" Good question. Let me answer it with a quote: "It's hard to find something when you don't know what you're looking for."

You might think these are the words of a sage, like The Buddha. Actually, they come from Officer Larry, the cop in the unintentionally hilarious cult movie classic *Plan 9 from Outer Space*.

I wrote *The Promise* to help you identify what you're looking for and then to help you find it. An ancient folktale illustrates what this book can do for you:

> There was once a beggar who spent his time sitting in his meager, unfurnished hut on his one piece of furniture: a beat-up wooden chest. The beggar sat on this crate, day after day for decades, wishing he were rich. One day, a traveler peered into the hut and saw the beggar perched on his chest, which she recognized at once.
>
> "Why are you sitting here in poverty?" she asked.
>
> "What else can I do?" bemoaned the beggar.
>
> "Don't you realize," replied the traveler, "that you are sitting on a grand treasure chest?"

The Promise of Your Best Self is your grand treasure chest. This book can help you not only recognize it but also open it. How can it do this? And how does it differ from other books?

The eminent mathematician John von Neumann once ended a debate with a colleague over a complex equation by telling him, "You're so far off, *you're not even wrong.*" This is how I feel about self-help and spiritual programs that promise authentic change via tortuous mystical or metaphysical routes that take you outside yourself.

The Promise doesn't send you scurrying around some nebulous "universe" like a rat in a maze, seeking Cheddar cheese. Which, in my opinion, is so far off that it's not even wrong. That's because right now, in this moment, you're perched on top of a fabulous treasure chest that contains a whole lot more than a chunk of Cheddar! All you need do is realize this, stand up, open it, and receive the treasure that is your birthright—Your Best Self. *The Promise* offers you a direct way to do this. If you're willing to put a little time and effort into You—not the elusive "universe"—your reward can be enormous.

How I Came to Write *The Promise*

Okay. You may like what you're hearing. So far, so good. But now two questions can naturally arise: "Who the heck is this guy?" and "Why should I believe he can help me?"

Both questions make total sense. After all, if you're going to put in time, work, and energy, you want to have at least an expectation that I can deliver. In my opinion, what you're really asking is, "Can I use this guy's pain for my own gain?"

My unequivocal answer? Yes.

Well, then, who am I?

Writing Credentials

I'm the author of two very popular meditation books, *The Best Guide to Meditation* and *8 Minute Meditation*. These books evolved out of thirty years of practicing meditation, beginning in 1975 when I was in law school. Believe me, my reason for starting was practical, not spiritual. In fact, the impetus for my entire meditation career was the heavy course load in the second year of law school, including Federal Taxation, the most dreaded requirement in the entire legal curriculum.

As the semester began, I quickly sank into the quagmire known as the IRS Code. Down, down, down I went. One day, by great good fortune, an alumnus of the law school appeared at an event promoting meditation as a tool for improving memory. Desperate for anything that might help, I immediately signed on for meditation instruction and began a twice-daily meditation practice.

The first time I meditated, I experienced something that, up until then, I had only a passing acquaintance with: *me*. It was as if I had finally slowed down long enough to meet myself. This newfound peace, coupled with the IRS Code, invigorated my determination to become a meditator. And I did.

Not only did I "ace" Federal Taxation, I became a life-long meditator. And I continued my meditation practice throughout a highly successful—and high-pressure—career as an attorney, marketing consultant, producer, screenwriter, and copywriter for some of America's foremost advertising agencies and motion picture studios, including Y&R and Paramount Pictures.

In the thirty years since graduation from law school, I have meditated every day, attended numerous silent retreats, and been fortunate enough to study and practice with some of the top meditation teachers in America in the Zen and Vipassana traditions.

I call meditation an "Eastern tool for Western results" that can result in lower stress levels, increased clarity, and greater focus. My audiences have included health-care professionals, mental-health workers, and church and civic organizations. In fact, if there were a Guinness World Record for "Most Attorneys Taught Stress Reduction in One Room," I set it when I taught meditation to six hundred lawyers in the Grand Ballroom of the Westin Palm Springs.

My two previous books, *The Best Guide to Meditation* and *8 Minute Meditation: Quiet Your Mind. Change Your Life,* evolved out of my real-life experience with the remarkable mental and physical benefits of meditation. The program and I have been featured in such mainstream magazines as *Cosmopolitan, Outside,* and on KCBS-TV in Los Angeles. Perhaps the best description of *8 Minute Meditation* comes from *Time* magazine, where it was called "the most American form of meditation yet."

"Street Cred"

What is equally important, if not more so, is my "street cred." By this I mean my personal—and hard-fought—journey to accept The Promise and My Best Self.

Although I am a meditation authority, that doesn't mean I float on a Buddha-like cloud 24/7. In fact, I have waged a lifelong battle with anxiety and depression. Over the years, I have learned to deal more skillfully with them, but there is no guarantee that they won't strike again.

I had always thought that my high IQ, schooling, and legal training would provide the rationality, reasoning, and insight that could help me overcome depression. Ironically, just the opposite proved true. Perhaps the best way to explain this is to invite you to return with me to those *"un*thrilling days of yesteryear"—2004, when my personal and professional lives were at low ebb. My "symptoms," as one of my meditation teachers told me, indicated that I was experiencing the classic "Dark Night of The Soul." But I was told not to worry: The Buddha taught that everything is "impermanent" and must, at some point, change.

I know my teacher was trying to be helpful. But my reply to him was, "Will this happen before the meter runs out? Because I'm all out of 'change.'" Ah yes, life was so grim back then that even pithy rejoinders like this couldn't lift my spirits.

But then, one ordinary day, unheralded, unexpected, and out of the blue, everything did change. . . .

There is a saying in meditation practice that "When

the student is ready, the teacher appears." And I was about to get lucky. In my case, my teacher was The Promise.

Encountering The Promise

It was early summer. I was driving on the freeway from Los Angeles to San Diego on my way to a convention in San Diego. I was already anxious, and a sudden freak summer rainstorm was making driving hazardous. I was becoming increasingly agitated and even considered turning around and going home.

About forty miles north of San Diego, an exit sign jogged my memory. A well-known retreat center was located here. Perhaps I might be able to sit down, try to calm myself there, and then decide whether to push on to San Diego or return to L.A.

I pulled off the highway, found the retreat center, parked, and entered onto a path that led to a verdant garden. The rain had stopped and the sun had reappeared. Compared to the gloom a few minutes prior, the sunlight seemed particularly dazzling.

I followed the path out onto a promontory several hundred feet above the Pacific. The view was breathtaking. The

Pacific Ocean spread out before me like an emerald green–turquoise carpet. Gentle surf folded itself toward shore, breaking in a small cove. Seagulls dallied overhead, languidly floating in the soft, warm breeze.

Still shaky, I sat down on a bench, shut my eyes, and tried to relax, using one of my meditation breathing techniques. After a few minutes, I sighed deeply, surrendering to the sound of the surf, the cries of the gulls, and the warmth of the sun. The breeze gently caressed my cheek. In that moment, I realized and surrendered to the fact that I could never think my way out of how I was feeling.

What happened next was unexpected and sudden. A direct experience beyond words. The best description I can give is that I suddenly found myself plunged into an ocean. Not the Pacific, but something vaster that seemed to contain the Pacific. There was someone, an "I," who was aware of this, *but it was not the same "I"* who had sat down on the bench ten minutes ago. This "I" was immersed in and yet simultaneously *contained* the vastness itself.

As this occurred, I had the thought, "Why am I not terrified by what's happening?" On the contrary, I had never been more at peace my entire life. Suddenly then I realized something amazing: I wasn't scared because this was *all familiar*—more familiar, in fact, than my own name. This "I" was who I had always been. Like the beggar in the story, I had been sitting on a treasure chest my entire life and hadn't realized it.

I sat a long time on that bench, simply breathing and effortlessly accepting my long-lost treasure. This required nothing more than my willingness. And when I finally stood up and headed for San Diego, I was drenched in my experience, a wonderful "afterglow" that lasted three days. I can't remember ever being at a convention where I had as much fun and effortlessly met as many new people.

Bringing The Promise Home

When I returned to L.A., I recounted my experience to two close friends, lifelong dharma buddies. When I finished, they just smiled and nodded. They, too, had encountered what I had begun to call "The Promise." Both of them suggested that it might make a great book.

At first, I demurred, insisting that it would be impossible for me to convey my direct experience of The Promise in words—much less provide a method that might help others experience it, too. But perhaps The Promise was insisting that it be shared. Because now, several years later, I am presenting it to you.

My Intention

The purpose of *The Promise* is to make you more "Promise-prone." Suffice it to say that when it's your turn, you will know it with a certainty that will negate any questions, doubts, and skepticism you might have ever had as to its truth.

When I first tasted The Promise, it was the most unreal *and* yet most real thing I ever experienced. I'll get into this "knowing," or *direct experience,* in more depth in the Concepts and Terms section on page 24. In the meantime, please know that I have done everything possible in *The Promise* to bring you to your own direct experience of it.

Also, please remember this: I share *The Promise* in the spirit of support and encouragement. I'm no superhero, just a regular Joe. I just happened to be the guy sitting on my treasure chest that sunny afternoon. And I want you to open your own.

The Promise

Reclaiming The Promise

You were not born into this world on some install-ment plan, like, "Great, I've got my feet and as soon as I can raise a little cash, I'll add a couple of toes." No, you came into this world a complete entity, a "pack-age deal," with organs, bones, limbs, lymphatic system, and a three-pound brain. Well, guess what? You'll find The Promise, as they say on TV, "included free in every package." This means that The Promise of Your Best Self is as real as your pinkie, even though you can't see or hold it—yet.

Why is The Promise included in every package? Let's assume for the moment that something vastly more powerful than you created you—call it God, the universe, consciousness, evolution, whatever you like. Given this, let me ask you: Do you think this "it," after it created you, would simply abandon you, without at least letting you "know" in some way that you're entitled to be alive and here? And I'm not talking about life at the low level of subsistence but life based in happiness that comes with the deep knowledge that *you are home.*

I believe this is so, and I think you would, too. In fact, here's my complete, detailed list of what you need to be entitled to receive The Promise:

Complete List of Qualifications Required to Accept The Promise

1. You were born.
2. You are currently breathing.

Tough requirements, huh?

The book you are holding is about one thing and one thing only—providing the tools you need to have your own direct experience of The Promise and to enter into Your Best Self.

Nobody Makes The Promise

One important thing to understand from the outset is that no person can make or give you *The Promise*.

Not me. My job is to give you understanding and tools.

Not you. This is not one of those miracle-diet pledge books where you *promise* that for the next fifteen days you will not eat Häagen-Dazs.

Not anyone. And I mean *anyone,* including gurus, talk-show divas, metaphysical authors, and "life coaches." If someone like that says they can give you The Promise, ask them if that shake comes with fries.

Bottom line. The reason that nobody can give you The Promise is that The Promise has already been kept. You own it. My job is to help you reclaim it. Your job is to be willing.

Reclaiming The Promise
of Your Best Self

The Promise is simply this: You already are Your Best Self. There is no "new you" you have to go out and find. As far as The Promise is concerned, you can't be a "new" you—because you already are Your Best Self. This means that you don't need to go looking outside of yourself for you, or to reconstruct, reshape, or rethink who "you" are. Isn't that a relief!?

In fact, when you allow yourself to listen, what The Promise is telling you, all the time, is this: You are the most perfect (insert your name) _____ there ever was, or will be, on this planet.

Where Your Best Self Resides

Imagine for a moment that you have not one, but two separate and distinct "minds." Let's call them "Thinking Mind" and "Working Mind."

Thinking Mind is the bustling 24/7 factory that creates your experience of the world. It produces a vast array of beliefs, concepts, judgments, and criticisms—a nonstop running commentary on what's happening in your life, moment to moment. Like all manufacturing operations, many "thought" products in Thinking Mind are flawed, inferior, and imperfect. But unfortunately, there are no quality-control inspectors to catch and toss them in a reject bin. And this is why so many of them get through.

Working Mind, in contrast to Thinking Mind, follows the old sneaker slogan, "Just Do It." It buys the food, pays the bills, answers the telephone, and a thousand other things—all without *thinking* about why it's doing them. Working Mind puts your keys in the car ignition, without thinking whether or not you like where you are going. It is dedicated to one thing and one thing only: doing what needs to be done. It makes no judgments or criticisms, and expresses no beliefs.

Working Mind is your unsung hero, forever overshadowed by Thinking Mind's deluge of thoughts, judgments, and beliefs. But that's okay—Working Mind is content to operate under the radar and allow Thinking Mind to do its thing.

Now don't let Working Mind's modesty deceive you: It is "home base" for Your Best Self, and much more than following the recipe for Aunt Tilly's chicken soup is going on here. Working Mind is the source of fresh insights, new perspectives, and simple yet elegant problem solving. It's also where Your Best Self resides. Since you begin coming from here, it's like getting a big chunk of your life back.

The Promise and Getting "Stuff"

The Promise isn't Aladdin, the Godfather, or the Tooth Fairy. It's not in the business of instant gratification, miracles, or wish fulfillment. Don't expect five bucks under your pillow. *Do* expect something much more authentic and powerful than you might ever imagine.

If getting "stuff" is what you think will make you happy, there are thousands of metaphysical programs, books, and gurus that guarantee you that if you *really, really* let the universe know what you want, it will deliver it to your door via some cosmic UPS truck.

But so what? Even if this were true—which it isn't—within an hour of getting your wish, you'll most likely have returned to the human condition's default position: discontented, bored, disappointed—*and already making your next wish*!

If you think that new Jag, job, or boyfriend will really make you happy, once and for all, you're welcome to stay with it. In my opinion, you're setting yourself up for continuous disappointment, unhappiness, and dissatisfaction.

Why?

Ask yourself this:

Do I prefer to waste my life begging for material handouts from some mystical/shmystical universe? Or do I want the kind of happiness that can never be taken away from me?

Make the latter choice—and let this book help you.

The Promise and Happiness

You were not born to experience misery and pain—even if you think or have been told this since childhood. As a human being on this planet, you have the absolute right to be happy.

As I've said, The Promise was already made and kept when you were born. It's been right here within you the whole time, patiently awaiting your acceptance of it. The only thing keeping you from the treasure of Your Best Self is the aspect of you I call "The Panel" (see page 13). Go beyond The Panel and you find yourself in Your Best Self.

What does this feel like? When you reclaim what is already yours, nothing changes—and *everything changes*. It's my intention to provide you the tools to experience this directly for yourself.

What Will Make You Happy Once and for All?

This is a big question. There are a gazillion books, talk shows, and self-appointed authorities out there in Medialand that tell you happiness is everything from figuring out the color of your parachute to plastic surgery. But after all is said and done, what is *really* going to do it for you? Where does *true* happiness reside?

The answer lies in a timeless truth, handed down by sages like The Buddha, philosophers like Seneca, and writers like Shakespeare. In four simple words:

Be who you are.

You've spent a lifetime erecting the Great Wall of China between who you think you are and who you truly are. It's time to whip out your jackhammer and demolish it—once and for all. Once you do, something amazing will reveal itself, something that might feel completely alien, yet paradoxically, something you realize you've known since you were born. *Welcome to The Promise of Your Best Self*. And for a small taste, try this:

1. Gently close your eyes.
2. Take a deep breath.
3. Silently repeat the words "I am."
4. Don't try to answer, complete a thought, or do anything else.
5. Sit like this for a few minutes.
6. Notice how you feel.
7. Open your eyes.

Your *Real* Wish List

Life is not a one-size-fits-all baseball cap. Each of us has his or her own conscious and subconscious list of what constitutes happiness—your *real wish list*. Here is mine:

- self-confidence
- ability to surpass negative thinking
- courage
- understanding
- self-sustainability
- connection

Do any of my wishes resonate for you? Could they be more substantial than a corner office, Porsche, or time-share in Cancún? Could life, lived in these wishes, help you, for perhaps the first time, be happy? Could this deep knowing of what you truly need actually increase your ability to get them?

The answer to all these questions is yes.

When you accept The Promise, you begin to live life authentically as Your Best Self, not as some counterfeit positive-thinking automaton who you know is just lying to you. Consider people who exude authentic confidence and smarts, and know how to get what they want and need out of life. Where does their power originate from? *From within.* You can be like them. In fact, you *are* them. Only you don't realize it—yet.

The Promise is designed to introduce you to the real you, the You you truly are: Your Best Self. As you work through the STOP, LOOK, and LISTEN Program, remember that The Promise doesn't promise to deliver material stuff. It promises much more.

Expectations and Results

Everyone wants speedy relief from suffering, pain, and challenges. Sometimes we even get it. But ridding ourselves of mental anguish and pain isn't as simple as popping an antacid for pepperoni pizza. What we're dealing with is something much more persistent: the human condition. Remember this as you work through *The Promise*.

Recognition and reception of The Promise will happen of its own accord. It's best not to think in terms of expectation. Actually, try not to think at all! When you drop expectations, *you get more than you ever expected.* Just follow the STOP, LOOK, and LISTEN Program. You'll enjoy the ride more and be pleasantly surprised.

2

Dealing with The Panel

As I've said, The Promise has already been kept: You already are Your Best Self. Whether or not you accept it is up to you. Of course I will do everything I can to help you do this, particularly with respect to the major obstacle to experiencing Your Best Self. I call it The Panel.

The Panel is another way to describe your ego, the continuous internal dialogue in your head that you know as "I." Sometimes it feels like you've got the entire cast of *The Producers* in there. Other times it's *Casablanca* or, on a bad day, *Apocalypto*.

Each of us has our own personal cast of Panel members. I give mine names. Here are a few of them:

- The Ruminator: A cross between Woody Allen and the Terminator who thinks everything to death—and is never able to make a decision.

- Einstein: A voice that tells me that I'm the smartest person in the whole wide world—brighter even than the cheerleading squad that won *Jeopardy!*

- Dolly: A male voice with a Tibetan accent who tells me I'm the kindest, most compassionate guy in the universe.

- Rick: The cynic, the skeptic, like Bogie in *Casablanca*—before Ingrid Bergman arrives. Always there when I listen to politicians. Or immediately after Dolly says something nice.

- El Stupido: The voice that reminds that me I am the biggest loser on the planet. It usually appears in tandem with the Ruminator.

Who's on Your Panel?

Now it's your turn. On the lines provided, write five of your Panel members. Don't be afraid that you're possessed, or have more personalities than Ben & Jerry ice cream flavors. It merely means you're just like everyone else.

This exercise will be fun and can help you put a name to the voice. It also helps greatly to know who you are listening to and how they might be keeping you from The Promise.

My Five Top Panel Members

_____

_____

_____

_____

_____

Not so bad, right? Do you see how powerful it can be when you actually LOOK at what's what? You'll be doing this much more in STOP, LOOK, and LISTEN.

The Panel's Job

Now that you've met The Panel, perhaps you're wondering what the heck it is doing in there.

The Panel's function is to interpret information from your physical senses and translate it into a truthful and accurate depiction of what is going on in your world. And that would be great—*if only it were true*! But most of the time, The Panel does exactly the *opposite,* through its main ploy, WYSIWYG (What You See Is What You Get, pronounced "wizziwig"). More about this on page 28.

Before you start trashing The Panel, you need to realize that it's simply doing its job. This means that, like everyone else with a job, The Panel seeks to make itself useful and indispensable so it won't get fired. There's only one problem: The Panel's goal is completely at odds with receiving The Promise.

The Panel has a vested interest in staying alive and living its "life." Even if that means making you miserable. Expecting The Panel to cease of its own volition is tantamount to asking a real person to commit suicide. Or, as Alan Watts, a famous meditation teacher, described it, "trying to pull yourself up by your own bootstraps." Maybe Horatio Alger characters did it, but try it yourself and you'll wind up flat on your *tush*!

The Promise doesn't ask you to perform the impossible. What you're going to learn in this book is to empower yourself, not to confront The Panel, but *to go beyond it*. In other words, you're going to send The Panel to unemployment! Because the truth is, you don't need The Panel to tell you who you are. *You already know.*

Empty Promises

Have you tried a mystical/shmystical program within the past six months? You know, one of those guaranteed metaphysical deals that promised you the moon—and failed to deliver even a pizza.

Don't be shy. Over the past twenty years, I've tried dozens myself. I divide them into three groups:

The Cosmic Pizza Hut. You select from the menu and order your wishes from the universe. Guaranteed delivery. But remember, if the universe fails to deliver, it's *your* fault! Programs like these are usually high in empty calories and amazingly low on results.

A Million Lists Will Set You Free. A compendium of nonstop, mind-numbing lists and exercises guaranteed to be your ticket to freedom, peace, material goodies.

Unfortunately, all your ticket usually buys is a one-way trip to frustration, confusion, and loss of hope.

This worked for me. And it will never work for you. Somebody has a "revelation" or epiphany that she wants or has been told by the universe to share with the world. Only one problem: There is no guarantee that what worked for someone else will work for *you*. In fact, there is no guarantee that what worked for her *even worked for her*!

Nevertheless, we buy the book, the CD, the software—whatever she's selling. We follow the instructions to the letter and wait for results. When they aren't forthcoming, we feel depressed, frustrated, angry, and, perhaps worst of all, guilty—courtesy of one of The Panel's favorite thought chains, which goes like this: "Dammit, it worked for her! There must be something wrong with *me*. I'm bad. I'm not doing it right. I don't deserve to be happy. I am a loser!"

Sound familiar? Why are we so ready to try these programs? Because we are paradoxical creatures. On the one hand, we aspire to be independent and wise. Yet we're also eager to turn our lives over to a total stranger who convinces us that she's "got it" and will tell us the secret of how we can get it. For a price, of course.

And what about *The Promise?* The following two lists describe what this book is—and is not—about.

The Promise *isn't* about

- metaphysical "laws"
- your inner child
- previous lives
- theology, religion, or dogma
- searching for secrets outside yourself
- "shoulds" that pressure you to change
- guarantees that can't be kept

The Promise *is* about

- accepting your birthright
- reclaiming Your Best Self
- down-to-earth, time-tested techniques you can easily do
- your innate power to transform yourself
- change that leads to your best possible life—and the contentment that comes with living it

How The Promise Program Works

The Promise is an authentic, powerful self-help book. Why? *Because you provide the "help."*

As I've said, success with The Promise requires you to do things. I encourage you not to lean, rely, or depend on me to get you where you already, deep inside, know you are. Think of me as your coach, not as a guru or authority figure. Someone who wants to assist you in reclaiming your true treasure—Your Best Self.

As your coach, I'm here for you every step of the way and will never leave you dangling out there on your own.

3

Preparation

What if I told you that you could transform your life simply by learning and doing a three-step safety slogan you learned back in the second grade: Stop, Look, and Listen. Believe it or not, the catchphrase designed to save your life at the age of seven can also change your life today, in a big way.

Okay, I see you out there, rolling your eyes, thinking, "Yeah, right." I know it sounds far-fetched, but please, just for a little while, be open to the possibilities of the power of STOP, LOOK, and LISTEN. Because **the**

most dangerous crosswalk in the world is inside your mind.

And it has to do with The Panel. Generating a non-stop flow of reckless and confused thoughts that are at the core of failed careers, marriages, and relationships. Not to mention depression, stress, and anxiety.

This table gives you an overview of how I've repurposed STOP, LOOK, and LISTEN to help you across the dangerous crosswalk in your mind.

STOP	Relax	Slow down the mind
LOOK	Inquire	Defog the mind
LISTEN	Attune to Your Best Self	Open the mind

STOP, LOOK, and LISTEN is your key to change. Let's take a few important minutes and become familiar with the program.

The Program

In the beginning, you will practice STOP, LOOK, and LISTEN techniques in 8-minute intervals. It's not a lot of time. In fact, 8 minutes is the time between two commercial breaks of *CSI* or *Oprah*. And can be a lot more rewarding.

All STOP, LOOK, and LISTEN techniques are simple, easy to understand, and clearly conveyed in step-by-step instructions. Each of the three steps is divided into sections designed to help you master it. They are:

Where you are: A brief review of what you might be experiencing at this point.

Where you're going: A reminder of where you're heading.

Techniques: The methods you'll practice.

Troubleshooting: "Technical support" on specific techniques and answers to commonly asked questions.

The STOP, LOOK, and LISTEN Training Schedule will show you how to begin to practice the three steps, combine them, and eventually incorporate them into an automatic habit. You'll find it on page 41.

You initially learn and practice STOP, LOOK, and LISTEN one step at a time. Then, you start combining STOP, LOOK, and LISTEN techniques. As you continue in this way, the distinction between the steps should gradually dissolve, replaced by a habit of STOP, LOOK, and LIS-TEN and connection to Your Best Self.

Concepts and Terms

Before you start the STOP, LOOK, and LISTEN Program, I want to familiarize you with some basic terms and concepts. While you may know what they mean in everyday usage, what they mean in *The Promise* is different. Don't worry if you forget them or are confused. I've already accounted for that in the materials and will repeat things along the way.

The Panel

You've already met The Panel. Nevertheless, it's important and worth reviewing again.

The Panel is the cast of thousands inside your mind, the virtual repertory company where each character has his or her own special voice and style of speech.

The Panel renders verdicts on virtually everything you do, judges and critiques the slightest action you take, and condemns perceived faults, mistakes, transgressions, and pratfalls in the most severe ways. Close your eyes and listen. It won't be long before you hear some of these voices, intoning what might be called their Top Ten:

1. "I should have done it."
2. "I shouldn't have done it."
3. "I deserve better."
4. "Life should be different."
5. "They're all out to get me."
6. "Nobody understands me."
7. "I want this to happen!"
8. "I can't let this happen!"
9. "I'm trying too hard."
10. "I'm too lazy."

The Panel dispenses zillions of thoughts and ideas, but all of them could be classified into three categories:

- happy/sad
- good/bad
- black/white

The Panel is always on patrol for any new ideas, concepts, and beliefs that threaten its existence. A primary way it polices things is by erecting a nonexistent but seemingly indestructible Barrier to Entry, which we'll be discussing in greater detail.

Bottom line? The Panel has made your mind a very crowded place with little space for Your Best Self. It's time for "spring cleaning."

The Barrier to Entry

In business, companies strive to create barriers to entry, ways they can bar competitors from their market. If The Panel were incorporated into The Panel, Inc., who do you think would be its major competitor?

Right! Your Best Self. Knowing who you truly are would force The Panel, Inc., into Chapter 11 in a heartbeat. So, to avoid this disaster, The Panel, Inc., creates the belief in you that you're unworthy of being Your Best Self. What does this barrier look like? Of course, it's not a physical thing that you can see. But you can *feel* it. Try this exercise:

1. Close your eyes and breathe naturally. Relax.
2. Remember something that you wanted to do in your life that would have made you happy, some-

thing you intuitively *really* wanted to do but never did. Think about this: *What prevented you?*

3. Take a long, deep breath, and relax. Try to identify that inner voice, the one with all the reasons why you couldn't do that thing. What is it saying? Does it have a familiar tone? It may be subtle, faint, or loud and strident. Don't try to respond to or dispel the voice. Just allow it to be there.

4. How do you feel when you hear this voice? Imprisoned? On the outside of life, your face pressed up against the window? Whatever comes up, just allow it.

5. Now, really look at this thought barrier to Your Best Self. Does it physically exist? Forget how it *feels*.

6. How would it feel if you dissolved this barrier? Can you do that now? If not, can you see how good it will feel when you do?

7. When you're ready, slowly open your eyes.

Barriers to entry in business last for only a limited time. That's because innovative competitors invariably come along with ways to break through them. It's the same with The Promise. No matter when your barrier was erected, how long it's been up, or how permanent you believe it is, STOP, LOOK, and LISTEN can help you break through it.

WYSIWYG

WYSIWYG (What You See Is What You Get) is an important concept. It's one of The Panel's favorite barrier tactics to convince you that you can never reach Your Best Self.

The English poet William Blake wrote, "If the doors of perception were cleansed every thing would appear to man as it is, infinite." In The Promise, we'll be less highfalutin' and call those doors of perception WYSIWYG. And cleansing them is what STOP, LOOK, and LISTEN is all about.

WYSIWYG is how The Panel creates a barrier between what is actually happening in your life and *what it wants you to believe* is actually happening. To get a taste of WYSIWYG, try this:

1. Sit comfortably and close your eyes. Relax.
2. Imagine yourself sitting on a bus on your way home from work. You're exhausted, tired, hungry, and cranky. You've got a splitting headache.

3. The bus doors open. A man with three young children climbs aboard. As the man pays the fares, the
   kids come tearing up the aisle, right up to your seat.
   One of them flings herself across you and plops into
   the window seat. The others leap into the seat behind you and start jumping up and down.

4. The kids are screaming at the top of their lungs.
   One kid's elbow strikes a glancing blow to your
   right temple as he swivels around. It doesn't hurt,
   but it makes your blood boil! You're close to being
   in a rage.

5. By now, the man has made his way up the aisle. He
   stops in front of you. You shoot him an unmistak-
   able dirty look. He looks at you and says, "Sorry
   about the kids. My wife is dying of cancer and
   we've just come from the ICU. The kids don't know
   how to handle it. Frankly, neither do I. Please for-
   give us."

6. Feel, *really feel* what's going on inside you as the
   man talks to you. Can you see how your interpre-
   tation of this event changes in an instant? Compare the thoughts, emotions, and feelings racing
   through you before the man spoke with you.

7. When you're ready, gently open your eyes.

Many people find this exercise to be an eye-opener. What about you? Are you starting to realize how you dwell in a world created by judgments, preconceived notions, and conditioning as to what you *think* is happening, as opposed to what is *actually* happening? Welcome to WYSIWYG, thanks to The Panel.

WYSIWYG might be the greatest obstacle to happiness ever created. If you've had enough, there is a way beyond it.

Going Beyond WYSIWYG

As I've said, WYSIWYG is shorthand for What You See Is What You Get. Here's a simple way to look at it, using an analogy to computer typefaces.

When you type in `Courier New`, what you *see* on your screen is `Courier New`. And that's exactly what you will get when you print it out. You can't type in `Courier New`, click Print, and expect **Ariel Black** to appear on your printout.

Similarly, the "typeface" of the world you are experiencing right now is the output of The Panel's input. How do you deal with it? Well, The Buddha said, "We are what we think. With our thoughts, we create the world." So the answer must be that if you change how you see the world, you change *your* world. No big deal, right? Insistent, negative, miserable, self-limiting thoughts? All you need do is not think them. Just think good ones.

Yeah, right! If it's so simple, how come you, I, and everyone else on the planet find it impossible to avoid self-limiting and negative thinking? But help is on the way: STOP, LOOK, and LISTEN offers you a powerful and direct way to remove the blinders preventing you from seeing what's really going on. Think of it as a kind of mental jujitsu.

As you begin STOP, LOOK, and LISTEN, you may start to see how pervasive self-limiting and negative WYSIWYG thinking detracts from your ability to live a full, happy life from the vantage point of Your Best Self. Don't feel dejected. Actually this is positive: For perhaps the first time in your life, you're in touch with how negative thoughts keep you imprisoned.

Core Beliefs

Core beliefs are incorrigible repeat WYSIWYG offenders: your most rigid, entrenched, and trusted ideas, concepts, judgments, and assumptions. Whenever you find yourself saying, "I can't help it" or "That's who I am," you're in the realm of core beliefs. Here's a short list of some of the most popular ones:

- I'm too old.
- I'm too dumb.
- My life should be different.
- I'll always be in debt.
- I'll never meet the right person.
- I don't have what it takes to succeed.

Core beliefs are another barrier to entry strategy used by The Panel and march in tandem with WYSIWYG. STOP, LOOK, and LISTEN can enable you to identify, challenge, and dispel these self-limiting and negative beliefs so that you can move on with your life—as Your Best Self.

Direct Experience

The term "direct experience" seems like a paradox: While you can't describe it with words, it's impossible not to know when you are in one.

Direct experience occurs not in Thinking Mind but

beyond it. You might say it's a pure, unobstructed, unadulterated dose of reality—life without The Panel. When you are *not* spinning a story or interpreting what is happening right now, then you're in a direct experience. I like to call it thinking from Your Best Self.

Although they elude verbal descriptions, direct experiences are by no means bizarre or mystical/shmystical. They are real and down-to-earth. You have them constantly, only you don't stop, put down your coffee cup, and think, "Hey, I just had a direct experience!" Here are a few common examples of direct experiences:

- watching a beautiful sunset and feeling completely connected with nature
- having the name of your new child suddenly "pop" into your head
- really tasting food
- knowing you should (or shouldn't) give a potential date your phone number

Try this simple exercise:

1. Sit alertly, but not rigidly. Gently allow your eyes to close. Take a couple of deep breaths. Relax.

2. Imagine that you've just completed a major project. You're physically and mentally exhausted. You just want to crawl under the covers and sleep for a year.

3. Allow yourself to feel this extreme mental and physical exhaustion. Don't fight it. Surrender to it. As thoughts arise, simply observe them. Remember, you're too tired to get involved. Let these thoughts arise and fade. Let everything just be as it is.

4. Now gently bring your attention to your breath. Experience what breathing feels like. Let go of everything but attention to your breath. If The Panel intrudes, remember, you're too tired to pay attention to it.

5. Just let go of everything and breathe.

6. When you're done, open your eyes.

What was your experience of just breathing? So tired that you couldn't listen to The Panel? Was it deeper, more "real"? Perhaps entirely new? This is direct experience. Common, everyday stuff.

Your Best Self

Your Best Self is the embodiment of The Promise: I call it "The Promise in Action."

When someone reports his first encounter with his Best Self, he's usually surprised at how different it is from his expectations. Comments like, "Is that it?" and "But I knew this all along!" are par for the course. But whatever his comments, he realizes he has gone beyond The Panel. And don't be surprised when it refuses to join in your celebration.

Remember, nothing threatens The Panel more than the direct experience of Your Best Self. And it will do its darnedest to convince you that this is just your vivid imagination, a delusion that "isn't good for you" and "will get you in trouble!"

When this happens, do your best to ignore The Panel. Go back to the last exercise and imagine yourself too tired to listen. You'll also find powerful techniques in STOP, LOOK, and LISTEN to silence The Panel. In time, Your Best Self can become a habit.

Receiving The Promise

At first blush, The Promise, like direct experience, appears to be yet another paradox: Why do you need to receive something that has already been given?

Comedians like to say that "Dying is easy. Comedy is hard." I'll rephrase it for our purposes: "The Promise is easy. *Accepting* The Promise is hard." Why? Because The Panel is determined that you not accept it. But the *real* you, Your Best Self, is always present, patiently waiting for you beyond The Panel's barrier to entry.

Remember, The Promise is that you already are who you truly are. This means that *failure is not an option*. The deeper you go into the STOP, LOOK, and LISTEN Program, the more Promise-prone you become.

4

The Promise Program:
STOP, LOOK, and LISTEN

STOP, LOOK, and LISTEN is a three-step program designed to empower you to break through and move beyond the self-limiting thinking of The Panel to a direct experience of The Promise of Your Best Self. Here's what it looks like:

STOP	Relax	Slow the mind
LOOK	Inquire	Defog the mind
LISTEN	Attune to Your Best Self	Open the mind

You need not memorize the table. Simply remember RIA—
Relax, Inquire, Attune.

Let's look at the individual steps of STOP, LOOK, and
LISTEN, how they relate to each other and to the whole.

STOP: Relax

STOP is the first step, and it's crucial. Practicing LOOK and
LISTEN without STOPping is like putting a car in gear with
the parking brake engaged: You'll get nowhere fast—and
need some new brakes!

As you begin to practice STOP techniques, you may
be shocked to discover how much of your life is spent in
a land called "Elsewhere and Elsewhen." You won't find it
at Disneyland but right where you are—or, to put it more
accurately, *aren't*.

Elsewhere and Elsewhen arises when your mind is
somewhere other than where you are. Let's say that you
are cruising down the freeway at 65 mph, thinking about
what to cook for dinner. Here's a typical monologue:
"Fish? Nah, we'll have it tomorrow. Chicken? Had it for
lunch today. Stew? Yeccch!" Eventually, the lightbulb goes
on: "Lasagna. Yes!" As it does, you return from Elsewhere

and Elsewhen to Planet Earth, where you realize that you've just driven ten miles past your exit.

It's a wonder we are all alive.

STOP techniques help slow down, relax, and rest your mind, enabling it to gravitate naturally to where you are right now. I call this "deceleration." When the mind decelerates, you are able to observe thoughts more clearly. When this happens, you're ready for step two, LOOK.

But please, don't interpret this to mean the complete cessation of the mind. After all, someone out there has got to drive!

LOOK: Inquire

LOOK is the investigative step in STOP, LOOK, and LISTEN, your internal Sherlock Holmes ferreting out the truth of those self-limiting, negative thoughts dished out by The Panel using its favorite play: WYSIWYG.

Like Holmes, LOOK trains a powerful magnifying glass on core and other beliefs, inquiring as to their truth. The process of inquiry is a powerful tool that can reveal the truth of your thoughts. The truth levels the playing field, removing The Panel's "home court" advantage. Once this starts to happen, it's time to bring in the big gun—step three, LISTEN.

LISTEN: Attune

In step three, LISTEN, you connect and attune with The Promise of Your Best Self.

Attunement is a direct experience. Although it can't be described in words, people want to know what this feels like. The following descriptions are guideposts:

- feeling the truth—not intellectually but in your heart
- feeling "at home" no matter where you are
- openness to and acceptance of whatever is happening
- surrender of resistance of control
- spaciousness
- the absence of anxiety, trepidation, or fear
- a "deep knowing" that you are Your Best Self

Sound good? You bet!

The STOP, LOOK, and LISTEN Training Schedule

I want to emphasize the importance of the continual, daily practice of STOP, LOOK, and LISTEN. If you merely read the techniques without doing them, it's the same as confusing a menu with the meal. And I don't want you to leave hungry.

To encourage and facilitate the practice of STOP, LOOK, and LISTEN, I've devised a simple training schedule that won't tax your time, patience, or energy. It's divided into four phases over a four- to six-week period and contains practice of each STOP, LOOK, and LISTEN technique by itself and in conjunction with its sister steps. In addition, I encourage you, beginning in Phase II, to move beyond the 8-minute practice session rounds as originally presented. You'll decide when.

The STOP, LOOK, and LISTEN Training Schedule is not a diet program or cookbook recipe that you must follow precisely to see results. This training schedule is flexible, intended to

- familiarize you with all STOP, LOOK, and LISTEN techniques

- give you a framework in which to sample, experiment, and develop different skills
- encourage STOP, LOOK, and LISTEN to become a habit—automatic, seamless behavior you never have to think about.

Here are some suggestions to help you optimize your STOP, LOOK, and LISTEN practice.

Environment. Find a quiet and private space. Reduce distractions, especially things that ring or beep (except your timer).

As I've said, 8 minutes is the time between two TV commercials. I've used this minimal attention span with great success in my book *8 Minute Meditation* and my Guided Meditation CD.

Remember, 8 minutes is your starting point. For the first week or so of STOP, LOOK, and LISTEN, remain here. After that, you can begin to increase your practice periods. The training schedule contains more information as to how to do this.

Posture. There are no rigid rules here. Simply sit in a way that is both comfortable yet alert. If you find yourself feeling more one way than the other, make appropriate adjustments. Some people sit on a straight-back chair. Others sit with their knees crossed. Some people need to lie on their back. This is all okay. Once you take your position and begin your session, don't change to another one. This is The Panel trying to take you off your game.

When to practice. Starting your day with a STOP, LOOK, and LISTEN practice session is a great reminder of The Promise. It is also an ideal way to develop consistency, which is integral to your success in building the habit of connecting to Your Best Self.

Consistency. In order to create a new habit of STOP, LOOK, and LISTEN, you must overcome your old habit of listening to The Panel, which won't go down without a fight! Let it know that you mean business and there is no better way to demonstrate this than by the consistent, daily practice of STOP, LOOK, and LISTEN.

Phase I

This is the getting-to-know-you phase of the training schedule. The goal is to gain familiarity with all of the STOP, LOOK, and LISTEN techniques.

Do each STOP technique for one 8-minute period. Use a simple device such as a kitchen timer. You can also use *The Promise Guided Meditation CD* (www.tastethepromise .com).

Do one or two techniques a day, but no more. If a technique resonates for you, you may do it twice in a row.

Don't rush this important initial step. This is not the Indy 500 but a journey that begins now and deepens over time. Practicing LOOK and LISTEN without first STOPping is like framing a house without first laying a foundation. Our goal is to lay a firm one. Make each 8-minute period the most important one in your life. Pay complete attention to what you're doing. Don't worry about "progress." That's a surefire guarantee that you won't make any.

Take at *least* one week to acquaint yourself with the STOP techniques. Don't be in a hurry to move on to Phase II until it feels right.

Phase II

After several weeks, you should be familiar with the STOP techniques and beginning to notice a deceleration in thinking. Once you feel this is happening, you're ready to bring LOOK into the equation. Here's how:

Familiarize yourself with the five LOOK techniques. Do each separately, one per day.

Once you are familiar with all the LOOK techniques, couple each one with a STOP technique. This means that each day you will do a STOP technique followed by a LOOK technique. Mix different techniques from each category. If any combinations seem especially strong to you, repeat them for a few days.

Play with these techniques for the next ten to fourteen days. Then ask yourself, "How comfortable am I feeling with combining STOP and LOOK?" One way to judge is by doing a STOP technique and noticing how clear you are when you inquire into your thoughts using your LOOK technique.

If you feel comfortable with STOP and LOOK, feel free to move on to Phase III, LISTEN. If you don't, that's fine, too. Stay with STOP and LOOK for a while longer. You'll know when it feels right to move on.

Phase III

This is where you integrate the three steps of STOP, LOOK, and LISTEN, which means that you are now the boss.

At this stage, you no longer use a timer and are free to remain with the individual STOP, LOOK, or LISTEN steps until you feel a natural inclination to move to the next one. And when you do:

Choose a single technique from the STOP, LOOK, and LISTEN sections.

Begin with your STOP technique and allow the sensation of relaxation to arise. When you feel it fully, relax even more, and on your exhale, allow yourself to transition into . . .

Your LOOK technique. Feel the sensation of awareness and presence arise. Allow this process of inquiry to arise naturally. As you begin to drop self-limiting and negative thinking, relax even deeper, accepting the shift into . . .

Your LISTEN technique. Allow attunement to Your Best Self to arise of its own volition. Steep in this feeling for as long as you like.

Phase IV

After three to four weeks, practicing STOP, LOOK, and LISTEN should seem natural and comfortable. You might also find that it automatically appe ars in your daily life.

This is a good indication that you have graduated to Phase IV.

In this phase, you need no longer follow the training schedule. Continue to deepen your habit and live your life in the continuous practice of STOP, LOOK, and LISTEN, attuned to Your Best Self. I call this phase on-the-job training; here is where you truly learn and assimilate the nuts and bolts of STOP, LOOK, and LISTEN.

Whenever you find that you've fallen prey to The Panel, don't be upset. These moments are most disturbing when The Panel pushes one of your buttons. This is to be expected and is a positive, affirmative indication: You're noticing that you feel "off" when you're not living in Your Best Self.

Whenever you realize that you are experiencing out-of-control thoughts, fearful feelings, shallow breathing, or any of The Panel's strategies, let that be your reminder that it's time to STOP, LOOK, and LISTEN. Use the Insta-Chill and Downshift techniques on pages 49 and 50. They come in handy anywhere and anytime you need to attune and reconnect with Your Best Self.

STOP, LOOK, and LISTEN
Operating Instructions

Before you begin the STOP, LOOK, and LISTEN Program, here are some short and simple "Operating Instructions."

Direct Experience Rules

When it comes to insights, experiences, feelings—anything that comes up in STOP, LOOK, and LISTEN—you are the final authority as to their validity, authenticity, and truth. This authority is the product of direct experience (see page 32). You don't need to consult friends, teachers, authorities, gurus, this book—or me. Look first and only to Your Best Self—and trust it.

Relax

This Operating Instruction might sound obvious, but it is vital to your success with STOP, LOOK, and LISTEN. You know from your own experience that it's difficult if not impossible to be grounded, aware, or trusting when you're frightened, wired, or agitated. That's why the first step of STOP, LOOK, and LISTEN is STOP, or relaxation.

Insta-Chill

Here's a quick and easy technique that you can add to your STOP arsenal.

1. Sit comfortably in a position that allows your chest and abdomen to move freely. Sit alertly but not rigidly.
2. Gently allow your eyes to close. Bring your attention to your chest and abdominal area. Notice your inhale. Notice your exhale. Do this for three breaths.
3. Now surrender control of your breath—just breathe without thinking about it. Feel a sense of release and relaxation that arises, and builds on each breath cycle.
4. Stay here for a few minutes. Open your eyes and feel the difference between before and after.

Downshift

Downshifting is something your auto's transmission automatically does when traveling up a steep grade and needs to trade speed for power. Downshifting in STOP, LOOK, and LISTEN enables you to deal with challenges in a similar way.

Let's say The Panel's got you tangled up in a particularly nasty web of mind chatter: Your thoughts are out of control, scattered, and confused, generating emotions like fear, anxiety, and depression. This is the perfect time to downshift to a lower gear. In the case of STOP, LOOK, and LISTEN your low gear is STOP. How do you do this? Start with your breath, which could be shallow, panting, or gasping. Take a long, deep inhale and just "sigh" it out. Do this one or two more times. Once you've settled down a bit, do a STOP technique.

As your body begins to relax in STOP, thoughts will start to slow down. This will allow you to observe your thinking from a calmer vantage point. Like Dorothy in the *Wizard of Oz,* you're pulling back the wizard's curtain. Once this occurs, you're ready to LOOK, to inquire into the thoughts that upset you. And when that feels right, you're on to LISTEN and reconnection with Your Best Self.

"Leave the Driving to Us"

I use this classic Greyhound Bus slogan to convey that there's no need to worry that I've left something out of the STOP, LOOK, and LISTEN Program that's vital to your success. So, if you are worrying that you'll be doing all this work for nothing—don't. *The Promise* you are reading is not the abridged version. I've taken everything you need for success and put it in this book.

Give Yourself a Break

This Operating Instruction is not New Age touchy–feel good cornpone but down-to-earth advice for success. Being kind to yourself is critical to accepting The Promise and connecting with Your Best Self, allowing you to see opportunities that you might otherwise miss.

> *Okay, are you ready to accept The Promise? To connect with Your Best Self? Then turn the page and begin to STOP, LOOK, and LISTEN.*

5

Step One: STOP

Where You Are

You're about to begin the STOP, LOOK, and LISTEN Program. Right now, you might be

- excited about the prospect of changing your life
- open to possibilities with no preconceived notions
- confused as to what this is all about
- wondering if STOP, LOOK, and LISTEN will work

- feeling like you're once again in for failure and disappointment

Whether it's any of the above or something else, don't worry; you're exactly where you're supposed to be, starting from exactly the right place for you. Let's begin by reviewing what STOP is about:

- STOP techniques work to decelerate and curtail the torrent of nonstop mind chatter.
- STOP techniques promote increased relaxation, clarity, and openness.
- STOP is the foundation of a strong STOP, LOOK, and LISTEN practice.

You can see that STOP is important in the scheme of things. So take your time, be attentive, and don't rush this step. You may say, "Oh, I'm a relaxed person. I'll just skip STOP and start with LOOK." This is not a good idea. Like I've said, skipping STOP and starting at LOOK is analogous to trying to frame a house without a solid foundation.

Let's review our STOP, LOOK, and LISTEN table:

STOP	Relax	Slow the mind
LOOK	Inquire	Defog the mind
LISTEN	Attune to Your Best Self	Open the mind

Where You're Going

You're going toward connection with Your Best Self. It's as simple as that.

STOP Techniques

Move Pen. Still Mind.

For this technique, you'll need

- a timer (which you'll be using in other STOP, LOOK, and LISTEN techniques)
- loose sheets of lined or unlined paper.
- a pen with smooth ink flow

1. Set your timer for 8 minutes.

2. Start writing. Don't think about what you're writing, just write down whatever enters your mind. Then do it again. And again. Even thoughts like "about what?" or "huh?" get written down.

3. Do not lift your hand from the page. Do not pause and reflect. Ignore punctuation, syntax, reasoning, logic, penmanship. Just do it. If your fingers cramp, stop, relax and flex them for a moment, and then continue.

4. Write down everything. Exclude nothing. If feelings of anger, embarrassment, or thoughts like "this is wacko" arise, write them down. Do not stop. Do not lift your pen to your lips and think "hmm."

5. If you find yourself asking, "*Who* is writing this?" allow the question and write it down. Then write about this question. If this question doesn't arise, don't worry.

6. As your hand moves, notice if any sense of separation between the "writer" and what is being written arises, even for an instant.

7. At some point, your writing may seem to flow automatically. Words will just appear. Don't stop

to search for their origin. Just allow writing to happen.

8. Continue to write until your timer sounds.

Close your eyes and take a deep breath. How do you feel? More relaxed than 8 minutes ago? Less relaxed? See if you can stay in touch with the "taste" of your experience.

TROUBLESHOOTING

Trying new things can be challenging. So having these issues—or any others—is to be expected.

I had the experience that I wasn't writing.
Who was?

At that moment, "you" weren't writing. In effect, there was no "who." The words emanated from awareness. What you were doing was playing stenographer—taking dictation from Your Best Self.

Should I reread or save what I wrote?

This STOP technique is not a journaling exercise. The exercise is centered on the experience of just writing, not the content produced. While there's nothing wrong with reviewing what you wrote, it is not relevant to and, in fact, might detract from your STOP, LOOK, and LISTEN practice. This is because The Panel loves nothing better than an opportunity to divert you with intellectual analysis and hidden meanings in what you wrote. Which can lead to questions, doubts, and confusion.

Of course, you are free to do whatever you like with your writing. If you feel it's worthwhile, save it. But for our purposes, you won't be using it further.

"Sipping" Breath

This sipping technique is simple; you did it as a child with your favorite drink. Now you're going "grow it up" in order to decelerate The Panel's thoughts.

Imagine a sweltering summer day. You've just finished some rigorous housework, gardening, or physical exercise. You are hot, tired, and thirsty. Someone hands you a tall, frosty glass of lemonade and a drinking straw. You plop the straw into the glass and begin to sip.

Now, we all know that if you sip a cold liquid too quickly, you're risking brain freeze, that searing pain that shoots between your eyebrows. That's why, even though you're parched, you know from experience to sip slowly through the straw. Remember to sip your breath in this way as you do the technique.

1. Sit in a comfortable position that allows your chest and abdomen to move freely. Sit alertly but not rigidly. Set your timer for 8 minutes.

2. Gently allow your eyes to close. Bring your attention to your chest and abdominal area. Notice your inhale. Notice your exhale. Do this for a few breaths.

3. Allow your jaw to drop slightly and pucker your lips, as if you were sipping through a straw. Your tongue may take on a natural concavity. Slowly take a "sip" of air. Relax. There is no need to force it. At the end of your sip, release and allow your breath to exhale naturally. Do this again. Two more times.

4. Now bring your attention to your thoughts. They might include the ever-popular "Am I doing this right?" or "What's the point?" or "I must look really stupid!" Whatever thoughts appear are fine. Try not to get involved with a thought or carried away by it. Simply return your attention to sipping breath.

5. Continue sipping breath, allowing thoughts, and returning to sipping breath until your timer sounds.

How does your body feel? More relaxed? Refreshed? How about your mind? Does it seem more relaxed, rested, or alert? Perhaps there's a sensation you might describe as "aerated"? Just observe. Don't judge or criticize yourself if these seem absent.

Buoyant Breathing

Breathing techniques are simple, direct, and powerful. Here's another one for your STOP arsenal. I do this technique every morning after I meditate and find that it simultaneously energizes me as it works to decelerate thoughts.

In Buoyant Breathing, you use your lower abdomen like a blacksmith's bellows, expelling air out of your nostrils. This technique is best done on an empty stomach. Try this warm-up to acquaint yourself with the technique:

1. Snort the air out of your nostrils, as though a small bug had flown inside them. It needn't be a forceful movement, just enough to expel a small fly.
2. As you expel air, feel the natural, bellowslike contraction of your abdomen and diaphragm. At the end of the expulsion, release and relax your torso.

Notice how letting go acts naturally to expand the "bellows."

3. Repeat a few times.

When you feel ready, try Buoyant Breathing:

1. Sit in a comfortable position that allows your chest and abdomen to move freely. Sit alertly but not rigidly. Set your timer for 8 minutes.

2. Gently allow your eyes to close. Bring your attention to your chest and abdominal area. Notice your inhale. Notice your exhale. Do this for a few breaths.

3. How connected to your breathing are you right now? Rate it 1 to 5, 5 being the highest.

4. Beginning with your next exhale, relax your stomach and abdominal muscles. Inhale deeply into your lower abdomen and begin to expel the breath in short bellowslike bursts by simultaneously contracting your diaphragm and abdomen as you snort out through your nose.

5. After ten expansion-contraction rounds, contract your stomach and gently lower your chin. Hold your breath for the count 1-2-3, raise your chin, and allow your breathing to return to normal.

7. Do two more rounds of this ten-breath cycle, pausing around fifteen seconds between each round. When you are done, sit quietly. Allow your breathing to return to its natural pattern. Remain like this until your timer sounds. Then gently open your eyes.

Bring your attention to the crown of your head. Do you notice tingling or other sensations here? How about elsewhere in your body?

Note the level of your awareness, as you did at the beginning of the technique. On a scale of one to five, what is it now?

Bring attention to your thoughts. Do they appear less intrusive? More? Something else? How about your surroundings? Are colors more vivid? Shapes clearer? Do you feel more grounded? More alert?

Cloud Hands

This is a simple Tai Chi Chuan technique that I do before I start to write and frequently between sessions. It takes just a few minutes, brings me back to earth, calms me, and helps STOP whatever The Panel is currently cooking up.

You can do Cloud Hands indoors or outdoors, any-where you can find a little space and good ventilation. If you initially feel self-conscious about the technique, do it in private. You'll soon get over any embarrassment. In fact, Cloud Hands is a great conversation starter; people always want to know what you're doing. And once you've told them, they usually ask, "Can you teach me?"

When you practice Cloud Hands, wear clothes that are loose enough to allow you to raise your arms overhead. It's also best to wear flat shoes or sneakers and work on a level surface. If at any time in the exercise you feel tired or your arms ache, simply stop. And when you're ready, begin again.

1. Set your timer for 8 minutes.
2. Stand comfortably, legs spread a little wider than hip-width. Bend your knees slightly. Anchor your-self. Bring your attention to your feet. Imagine that the soles of your feet are rooted to the earth. Let your arms be loose and relaxed, dangling at your sides.
3. As you inhale and exhale, notice the movement of your diaphragm.
4. Slowly raise your arms, elbows slightly bent, palms facing down. Let your wrists drop and fingers

relax. Continue this movement upward until your arms are at shoulder height.

5. *Slowly* begin to make circles with your arms. One arm moves clockwise and the other arm moves counterclockwise. As your arms describe opposing circles, continue to relax your hands and wrists.

6. As circling becomes more comfortable and automatic, bring your attention to your chest. Notice the presence of any energy, tingling, or vibration. Also check your palms, hands, wrists, and arms. Are there any such feelings present? Just observe and note sensations and feelings. If you sense nothing, that's fine.

7. As you continue your movement, scan your body for feelings, the ebb and flow of energy, anything you notice, including places where your energy—called chi—appears blocked, stuck, or "yucky."

8. Shift your attention to the space surrounding you. What does this feel like? Warm? Friendly? Like gliding through maple syrup?

9. Bring your awareness to your thoughts. Are they softer, slower, less important, less insistent? Perhaps, for the moment, not present at all? Just observe.

10. If your arms become tired, lower them and stand quietly, noting energy flow, weary wrists, tight back—whatever is present. When you're ready, begin again.

11. When your timer sounds, gently lower your arms and let them hang loosely at your sides.

Take a body scan, starting at the top of your head and moving down to the soles of your feet.

How are you feeling? More peaceful? More open? More present? "Lighter"? Is there any pleasant energy flowing through your limbs and torso?

TROUBLESHOOTING

When I did Cloud Hands, I felt my thoughts fade into a kind of "background." It felt like I was more "here." Is this okay?

It's more than okay. You're describing a view of this present moment unobstructed by The Panel. While Cloud Hands is simple and easy, it has the power to initiate profound contact with Your Best Self.

Hot Spots/Cool Spots

This technique can empower you to "chill yourself out" at any time, leading to increased clarity, perception, and the deceleration of self-limiting and negative thinking.

This technique uses the analogy of thermography, the diagnostic tool that creates a colored "map" of temperature variations. You've seen thermographic images on medical shows, *CSI*, and weather radar. Typically, blue and green indicate cool spots, whereas orange and red indicate hot ones.

In Hot Spots/Cool Spots, you create a thermographic scan of your body, noting "cool spots" and "hot spots." You then convert hot spots and hot thoughts to cool spots and cool ones.

An example of a cool thought is the image of you lolling on a chaise lounge on a beautiful beach in Hawaii. A hot thought is the image of that argument with your boss or spouse yesterday. In this technique, you will "transfer" the experience of your cool thought to your hot one.

If you're confused, don't worry. As you do the technique, you'll see how this all fits together.

1. Sit in a comfortable position that allows your chest and abdomen to move freely. Sit alertly yet comfortably. Set your timer for 8 minutes.

2. Gently allow your eyes to close. Bring your attention to your upper torso. Observe your inhalations and exhalations for a few breaths. Notice the breath naturally settling down.

3. Visualize yourself lying on your back on an X-ray table. Starting from the top of your head, imagine that you are doing a thermographic scan on your body. Slowly scan downward, noting places that feel cool, hot, and anything in between. Assign colors to these spots: blue and green for cool spots, orange and red for hot ones.

4. Scan slowly. No area is too small or insignificant. Be comfortable in these areas—and your body. Do not be concerned with doing this perfectly. This is a STOP technique, not a medical examination.

5. When your scan arrives at the soles of your feet, rest for a moment. Now allow your attention to be drawn to a cool spot. Get acquainted with how it feels. You might see colors, feel vibrations, or even taste flavors. There's no need for words. Just feel.

6. Now allow your attention to be drawn to a hot spot. It might feel more unpleasant than the cool spot. Try not to compare, judge, or evaluate it. Just feel it.

7. Bring your attention back to your cool spot. Reconnect with how it feels. See if you can "transfer" these cool feelings back to your hot spot. Do your best to allow the sensations of your cool spot to permeate, suffuse, and cool your hot spot. As this happens, visualize its colors changing from red or orange to green or blue.

8. Now you're going to apply the same procedure to thinking. Bring your attention to your thoughts. Choose one as it arises, and notice if it feels hot or cool. When you find a cool one, experience how it feels. Next, find a hot thought and do the same. Now return to your cool thought and transfer its cool feelings and sensations to your hot spot and allow them to suffuse it.

Continue to practice in this way until your timer sounds.

How do you feel in your body? In your mind? More relaxed? More available to what's happening in this moment? Allow cool feelings of relaxation and tranquility to permeate your body and mind as you move back into your daily activities.

French Press

In this technique, you are going to create a "mental French Press" that you'll use to filter self-limiting and negative thinking out of your system.

You're probably familiar with these glass or stainless-steel cylinders with a plunger/strainer device. To make coffee, you put ground coffee into the cylinder, add hot water, cover the cylinder with the plunger device, and plunge the filter to the bottom of the cylinder, forcing the coffee grounds to the bottom. This leaves clear, fresh-brewed coffee above the filter, and grounds below.

Let's do the same thing—with you as the French Press and The Panel as the coffee grounds.

1. Sit in a comfortable position that allows your chest and abdomen to move freely. Sit alertly but not rigidly. Set your timer for 8 minutes.
2. Gently allow your eyes to close. Bring attention to your chest and diaphragm. Notice your inhale and exhale. Do this for a few breaths.

3. Imagine that you are a clear glass cylinder containing self-limiting and negative thoughts and feelings, represented by black "thought granules" suspended within it. Visualize a large plunger/strainer hovering over your head. Allow it to *slowly* sink down through the cylinder, gathering those black granules in front of it and forcing them downward. As this happens, let go of all thoughts and body sensations.

4. Follow the movement of the plunger from the top of your head down through your throat, chest, torso, and legs—all the way to the soles of your feet. As thought granules filter down, notice any sensations of openness and spaciousness left behind. Don't describe these sensations; simply feel them.

5. When the plunger/strainer arrives at the soles of your feet, take a deep breath and imagine your soles as two porous surfaces. Allow the plunger to gently push the accumulated sediment through your pores and out of your body.

Remain relaxed until your timer sounds.

How do you feel? More relaxed? Peaceful? Is there less mind traffic? Have any aches and pains disappeared?

What would it be like to stay in this feeling throughout your day?

TROUBLESHOOTING

I never had this many thoughts before doing STOP. Why?

There's an old saying: "Don't kill the messenger."

STOP techniques don't cause an increase in thinking. In fact, what is happening is just the opposite: You're not thinking more than you normally do, but noticing, perhaps for the first time, *how much thinking you actually do!*

Your question indicates that you're doing great—and beginning to see the truth that The Panel doesn't want you to see. The culprit here isn't STOP, it's The Panel, trying to convince you that STOP techniques aren't good to do and could lead to disaster, like greater clarity, focus, serenity, and—heaven forbid—Your Best Self! Now we don't want that to happen, right?

Wrong!

If I STOP, how will I get things done?

When you STOP, not only do you get things done, you get more done in a better way.

We are a society of doers. And somewhere along the line we bought into the belief that relaxing and letting go of stressful, unneeded thinking is a downward spiral to hell, and means losing our drive, our jobs, and winding up an unemployed coach potato watching *I Love Lucy* reruns.

The truth is exactly the opposite: The more you experience your natural tendency to relax your mind and body, the more effective, competent, and resourceful you can be.

At this point, you have practiced STOP for more than a week. Have you found yourself afterward in an enervated condition, lying around like a lump? Or have you found yourself perhaps calmer, clearer, and looking forward to what you need to do next? I'm willing to bet it's the latter. This is how life can be when you're not bogged down in a litany of nonstop self-defeating, self-limiting mind chatter—that bonfire of unneeded stress and tension fueled by The Panel.

Bottom line: STOP doesn't stop you. *It starts you—* toward The Promise of Your Best Self.

I'm learning how to STOP. Now what?

Now it's time to LOOK.

You've come a long way with STOP and established a firm foundation for LOOK and LISTEN. It's time to take an in-depth look at the contents of your thoughts and see just how truthful and in your best interests they really are. Get ready: You may be in for a shocker.

6

Step Two: LOOK

Where You Are

Congratulations! For the past several weeks, you've been practicing relaxing and decelerating thinking with STOP techniques. Doing these techniques once or twice is great but no guarantee that you're forever going to be free of racing thoughts, agitation, and anxiety. You are, however, on the road to cultivating skills to deal with them, as well as accumulating valuable "frequent-flier miles" toward attuning to Your Best Self.

I applaud your success with STOP. But why settle for

a gold star when we're really going for the gold that awaits inside your treasure chest: The Promise of Your Best Self. LOOK is the second step on the way.

Where You're Going

In STOP, LOOK, and LISTEN terminology, LOOK is not about the sense of sight but rather about inner vision, the ability to *see beyond* The Panel's self-limiting, negative beliefs, judgments, and opinions. LOOK is about this kind of inquiry, the examination of thinking and thoughts in the clear light of truth. Here's our table again:

STOP	Relax	Slow the mind
LOOK	Inquire	Defog the mind
LISTEN	Attune to Your Best Self	Open the mind

LOOK is about presence, the shift from Elsewhere and Elsewhen to Right Here, Right Now—and closer to The Promise of Your Best Self.

Here's an illustration of what I mean. Imagine that you're driving down a rain-slicked, windy road on a humid summer night. You're late for an important event. The inside of your windshield keeps fogging up. You're distracted by your lateness and don't realize you're over-driving, going at a faster speed than your headlights can handle. Then, suddenly, you do. What do you do next?

A. Speed up

B. Maintain speed

C. Slow down

D. Turn on your defroster.

E. A and D

F. B and D

G. C and D

Of course, the answer is G. You need to both switch on your defroster *and* slow down. In STOP, LOOK, and LISTEN, slowing down corresponds to STOP; defogging your windshield is comparable to LOOK.

"I love Paris in the spirngtime."

Huh?

I slipped that sentence in to illustrate that defogging your windshield isn't so simple. Did you catch the typo? Most people don't. This is because throughout your life, you've read, hummed, or heard the song "I Love Paris in the Springtime" so often that your mind has pre-judged what the sentence really says.

This is another example of WYSIWYG at work. Unfortunately, the process goes way beyond this typo; it's a metaphor for the myriad preconceived notions and concepts—the *"misspellings"* The Panel keeps alive inside you, resulting in constantly *misreading* events, conversations, and relationships, often with negative consequences to you and the people close to you.

So how can you level the playing field and beat The Panel at its game of misdirection and deception? You need to LOOK. The following techniques are here to help you do this.

LOOK Techniques

"Is It Live, or Is It Memorex?"

This classic advertising slogan used in the '60s Memorex recording tape TV commercial provides a bird's-eye view of the subterfuge created by The Panel to keep you from being present.

In the commercial, singer Ella Fitzgerald is in a recording studio, standing before a microphone. She sings a note that is so high it shatters a nearby wineglass! Next, a recording of Ella singing this note is played back on Memorex tape. And guess what? *It shatters another wineglass!* A voice-over asks: "Is it live, or is it Memorex?"

Your inability to distinguish "live" from "Memorex" thoughts may be keeping you from living life from Your Best Self. Think about The Panel's nonstop litany. Are these thoughts happening now, or are they merely replays and repetitions of the past? When you do this LOOK technique, you might find the answer surprising.

1. Sit in a comfortable position that allows your chest and abdomen to move freely. Sit alertly but not rigidly. Set your timer for 8 minutes.

2. Gently allow your eyes to close. Bring your attention to your chest and abdominal area. Notice your inhale. Notice your exhale. Allow it to naturally settle down.

3. Bring attention to your thoughts. Notice how they arise, linger, and then fade away, immediately replaced by new ones.

4. Choose the next thought that presents itself. Label it "Memorex" or "Live." Remember, "Memorex" is a

thought you've had in the past. "Live" is a thought that feels fresh, alive, and newborn.

5. If a Memorex thought is particularly strong, pause and bring attention to body sensations. Note the presence of any familiar emotions. What are they? What do they feel like? Do they trigger more Memorex thoughts? More Memorex body sensations?

6. Next, repeat the previous process with a Live thought. Note the presence of familiar or new feelings and emotions. What do they feel like? Note how they feel, the sensations they trigger, and whether new Live thoughts and feelings arise.

7. Compare your Live versus Memorex experiences. Which seems more familiar: Memorex or Live? There's no reason to ask why. Simply look.

8. Repeat the process until your timer sounds.

How do you feel? Are you more present? More "Live"? Are you more "Memorex"? Maybe both.

Core Beliefs and Memorex

The most common category of Memorex thinking is probably the core belief (defined on page 31). These "blasts from the past" can be pernicious energy vampires. For instance, take the core belief "I'm not good enough." This self-limiting and defeating belief is the epitome of Memorex thinking. It's so highly developed in most of us that it has become automatic, constantly flying under the radar, imprisoning us in a fictional prison.

On the opposite end of the spectrum is Live thinking—original, fresh, and new, untainted by your past beliefs, concepts, and judgments. When you take a close LOOK at your self-limiting concepts and core beliefs, you see them for what they truly are: *untrue*. When this occurs, these negative thoughts dissolve into the thin air they emanated from, leaving behind more spaciousness to accommodate Live thinking, a way of being that is a truly authentic. You already know it as Your Best Self.

TROUBLESHOOTING

Can I convert thinking from Memorex to Live?

Yes, but not by suppressing Memorex thoughts, but by *surpassing* them.

Considering that you've got a lifetime of Memorex tapes running, it's a wonder there's any room left at all for Live thinking. And harboring the expectation that you will be able instantly to clean house is unrealistic and merely another Memorex tape! This does not mean, however, that it's impossible.

Practitioners of aikido, Tai Chi Chuan, and other martial arts use their opponent's energy to defeat them. You can do the same with Memorex beliefs. When you stop resisting The Panel's incessant assault and allow it, you amazingly can find yourself beyond it, engaging in Live thinking and realizing The Promise of Your Best Self.

The Trial

In this LOOK technique, you will investigate the truth of painful and self-limiting thoughts and core beliefs. It's a courtroom drama, complete with prosecutors, defenders, judge, and a jury—all played by you!

Here's how it works: You choose a core belief and place it on trial and then proceed to make pro and con arguments as to its truth or falsity. After opposing arguments, the case goes to the "jury" (you), who weighs the evidence employing the classic reasonable doubt legal standard. If the evidence is found untrue, the verdict is not guilty; if true, guilty.

In a court proceeding, the reasonable doubt standard

requires that a jury try to create an alternative scenario to the facts presented at trial. If they come up with one, it raises "reasonable doubt" as to the accuracy and veracity of the testimony—requiring a not-guilty verdict.

The following example should help you do this technique.

Get a sheet of paper and divide the page into four columns. Give each column a heading, like so:

Belief	Prosecution evidence	Defense evidence	Reasonable doubt that this belief is true?

Let's suppose that you hold the core belief "I have no self-confidence." Enter this under the "Belief" column.

Now assume the role of prosecutor. In column two, introduce all the "evidence" you can summon to "make the case" that you have no self-confidence. Does this DA seem familiar? He should: It's The Panel.

Once you've completed the "Prosecution Evidence" column, the State rests. Take a few slow, deep breaths and relax. How are you feeling? Are you angry, hot under the

Belief	Prosecution evidence	Defense evidence	Reasonable doubt that this belief is true?
I have no self-confidence.	I didn't stand up to my mother.	I stood my ground and didn't change my plans to suit hers.	Yes. Not guilty.
	I clam up at parties.	I had a nice talk with that cute guy at that art opening. I was the one who initiated contact.	Yes. Not guilty.
	I haven't been asked out in months.	Didn't that new guy from payroll ask me to lunch last Tuesday?	Yes. Not guilty.

collar, hopeless? You might not be feeling terrific about The Panel's accusations. But look on the bright side: Now it's your turn to defend yourself and blow The Panel's case out of the water!

Under "Defense Evidence," enter all your evidence that refutes and proves the DA's evidence untrue. Also, enter any *new* evidence that undermines his allegations. Some facts will come to you right off the bat. Some will appear out of the blue. Don't think about where they came from, just use them! The more the better.

Once you have finished column three, the defense rests. Now how do you feel? Many people report feeling empowered by their ability to defend themselves, challenge these assumptions, and take the offensive.

Now the case goes to the jury, who will weigh the evidence against the reasonable doubt standard. Remember, if there is a reasonable alternative scenario to the facts presented at trial that might prove that the defendant is not guilty, the jury is required to return a verdict of not guilty.

In our example, the core belief on trial is "I have no self-confidence." Let the jury examine the arguments on both sides, one by one, using columns two and three. The first evidence for this being true is in column two, where it is alleged that you didn't stand up to your mother. But column three contains a verifiable instance where you *did* stand up to her. Same for not being asked out and initiating contact at the art opening.

These facts present alternate scenarios that cast reasonable doubts as to the truth of the statement, "I have no self-confidence." They are strong evidence to the contrary—that you *do* have self-confidence. Good. You're beginning to get closer to the truth. In column four, you enter yes all the way down the column, meaning that . . . *The jury finds you not guilty! Congratulations!*

Don't be surprised when you get a not guilty verdict even when you originally thought yourself guilty. It's amazing how not guilty you really are, almost all the time.

After the verdict, take stock of how you're feeling. People report feeling relief, exhilaration, and freedom from The Panel. Some even laugh at themselves for having harbored "that ridiculous idea."

Keep this sample handy when you do The Trial.

Unlike other STOP, LOOK, and LISTEN techniques, The Trial takes more than 8 minutes to practice. Don't think you're wasting your time. This technique provides a powerful perspective as to how The Panel operates and how wrong it can be.

Now it's your turn to try it yourself. You need a copy of a table set up with the following columns. You can keep the earlier example by your side for reference.

Belief	Prosecution evidence	Defense evidence	Reasonable doubt that this belief is true?

1. Follow the procedure as discussed. Fill in the columns sequentially, starting with your belief. Work your way through evidence for and evidence against this belief.

2. In the "Reasonable doubt" column, place yes or no in each box.

3. Examine the results and render the verdict. Do you have more yes than no responses? Then you're not guilty. Fewer? Then the verdict is guilty.

Was the verdict not guilty? Probably. How do you feel right now? Relieved? Surprised? Perhaps excited? You're beginning to tap into the power of inquiry, of LOOK, and using it to prevail over false core beliefs.

Was the verdict guilty? If so, go back and examine

your defense evidence. Can you introduce any new evidence to help your case? Relax and see. You may be surprised at what you missed. When new evidence appears, "reopen" the trial and do the technique again.

"Does It Serve Me?"

This next technique enables you to evaluate The Panel's nonstop barrage of thoughts in terms of perceived versus actual merit. It's a good opportunity to start the long-overdue spring cleaning of your "mental attic." What may seem a chore at first can lead to newfound openness and spaciousness, creating, "breathing room" for The Promise of Your Best Self.

Here's a simple rule of thumb to identify thoughts that serve you from those that don't:

A thought serves you when it

- motivates positive action
- elicits positive feelings—toward yourself and others
- expresses love—for yourself or another

A thought does *not* serve you when it

- induces irrational mental anguish, suffering, and pain
- arouses indecision, inaction, or paralysis
- Propels you into Elsewhere and Elsewhen

1. Sit in a comfortable position that allows your chest and abdomen to move freely. Sit comfortably but alertly. Set your timer for 8 minutes.

2. Gently allow your eyes to close. Bring your attention to your chest and abdominal area. Notice your inhale. Notice your exhale. Do this for a few breaths.

3. Bring your attention to arising thoughts. When a particular one generates upset, pain, or dis-comfort, don't try to censor or suppress it. Instead, rest your attention on it and simply observe the feelings and emotion generated. See if this thought also initiates a domino effect, triggering more negative thoughts and feelings. Don't be upset. Don't resist. Just allow. Do this for a minute or two.

4. Ask yourself, "Does this thought serve me?" Sit quietly. Allow the question to be there without a need to have an answer. That will get The Panel

involved. And you don't need it. Be patient and LOOK at the question. Give it the space and respect to answer itself. Sit quietly until you "feel" an answer. It will probably be no. Remain like this for a few minutes. If an answer doesn't appear, don't worry. It's not a problem.

5. Return your attention to thinking. When an arising thought generates pleasure, joy, or well-being, don't grasp at it. Simply rest your attention on it and observe your feelings and emotions. It, too, may initiate a domino effect, triggering positive thoughts and feelings such as pleasure, well-being, love, or peace.

6. Observe this thought and ask yourself, "Does this thought serve me?" Sit quietly. Allow the question simply to float. Don't try to answer it with the mind. The answer will come from a much truer place. Allow the question to answer itself. It most likely will be yes.

7. For the next minute or so, feel this openness. If you like, repeat the "Does it serve me?" inquiry. Remember, you are not seeking an answer as much as allowing the question to "be"—and *answer itself*.

When your timer sounds, turn it off and check in with yourself. How do you feel? Are you able to see how inquiring into self-limiting and negative thinking negates and dissolves it? Did you notice how false beliefs can create the domino effect of suffering? How about pleasant and positive thoughts? What do they feel like when they "serve you"? Is it possible that The Panel has overshadowed, conditioned, and confined your thinking your entire life, keeping you from The Promise of Your Best Self?

TROUBLESHOOTING

If negative thoughts don't serve me, why do
I have so many?

Once you begin to LOOK at your thinking, you will most likely be shocked at the high percentage of negative, self-limiting, and unhelpful thoughts you have. Questions like this are unhelpful and are just another ploy by The Panel to keep you from living the main event—your life. See for yourself. Starting right now, LOOK at the truth of your thinking—and realizing how much The Panel has "gamed the system."

Einstein said, "One cannot solve a problem with the same kind of thinking that gave rise to the problem." Let go of The Panel's kind of thinking and you not only solve the problem, you meet The Promise of Your Best Self.

Fun with Dick and Jane

Remember Dick and Jane? They were the baby boomer generation's first celebrity couple—even before Tom and Nicole! Who can forget their exciting journeys, walks in the park, hill climbs, and trips to the well (do any still exist?). And while we hung out with Dick and Jane, this plucky twosome helped teach us to read. We weren't ready for Shakespeare. What we needed was a primer, and we got one.

You don't find a lot of adverbs and adjectives in Dick and Jane books. "Look, Dick. Do you see the tree?" "Yes, Jane. I see the tree." You won't find Dick asking Jane if the tree is deciduous or a maple. Nope, it's simply "tree."

Now, it's time for you to do the same thing. You're going to take a walk down your street and conduct your own Dick and Jane narrative, describing what you see exactly as they would, using only nouns.

Here's a sample of what your narrative could look like:

Car . . . fence . . . tree . . . flower . . . dog . . . car . . . bird . . .

Sounds simple, right? Well, get ready. You may be in for a big surprise. We'll discuss this after your walk.

Find a location where you can walk safely, slowly, and undisturbed for 8 minutes. You might not reach the end of your block in that amount of time. And if you do, don't cross any streets. Just turn at the corner, or turn around, and continue.

Take your time and walk slowly. Describe all objects by nouns *only*. Forget that adjectives and adverbs ever existed. A truck is simply a "truck." Not "big," "my," or "FedEx."

1. Take your timer and go to where you'll be walking. Set your timer for 8 minutes.
2. Bring your attention to your chest and abdominal area. Notice your inhale. Notice your exhale. Do this for a few breaths. Stand erect but not at rigid

attention. Feel relaxed and alert. Feel the earth beneath your feet. Allow yourself to feel supported
and grounded.

3. Bring your attention to seeing. Allow your eyes to
   relax so that you're not staring at objects so much
   as allowing them to come into your visual awareness. In other words, make them "soft."

4. Begin slowly walking down the block. Feel
   grounded. After a minute or so, take notice of your
   surroundings. Label what you see. Remember,
   nouns only: "tree . . . car . . . boy."

5. Keep it simple. When you find yourself thinking,
   judging, describing, or elaborating, just realize this
   and return to one-word noun definitions. If you're
   hijacked by thoughts such as, "car . . . is this the
   new Honda?" pause and take a breath. Reconnect
   with your feet and get grounded. Then, without
   judgment, continue your walk until your timer
   sounds.

Stand quietly for a minute or so. How do you feel?
More relaxed? More aware? Tense? Exhausted? What's
it like to LOOK at things simply as they are, without adding tons of thinking? Did you experience them

more deeply, more clearly? This is pure LOOKing"—
reality, unencumbered by thoughts about it, and without
the trappings of The Panel. This is home base for Your
Best Self.

TROUBLESHOOTING

*I was having a nice stroll with Dick and Jane,
until a yapping Yorkie made me lose it.*

The German philosopher Friedrich Nietzsche said, "What
doesn't kill me makes me stronger." Kind of a Teutonic
forerunner to, "When life gives you lemons, make lemonade."

When a strong challenge to presence arises, like the
barking dog, see it not as a hindrance but an opportunity.
That yapping is reminding you that you are not present
and LOOKing.

If the slings and arrows of daily life were a Starbucks
drink, we might call it Hot-Button Grande, HBG for
short. And it would sell out every day! One of my pet
HBGs is finding abandoned supermarket carts propped up
against my front fence. When I see one, my thought isn't
"metal," "cart," or anything like that; it's the unprintable
variety.

You probably have your own HBGs. The inconsiderate next-door neighbor who parks her forty-foot Winnebago in the driveway, creating a lovely view from your living room window. Your gardener blasting a 56 dB leaf blower in your ear, even though it's illegal. I'm willing to wager that somewhere in your 8-minute Dick and Jane stroll, you were yanked away from "tree" and into a favorite HBG.

How in the world can you make lemonade in the midst of all these lemons? By LOOKING: When you LOOK, you are present. And when you are present, you understand that Your Best Self has already mixed up a big pitcher of wonderful lemonade called Life. How do you get your taste of it when an HBG strikes? Downshift into a STOP technique. Calm down. Relax. And when you're ready, have a LOOK.

I can't get the hang of LOOK.

When people report having trouble with LOOK, it usually indicates that the challenge is "upstream," in STOP.

LOOK is about inquiring into the truth of what is going on in this very moment. And it helps to be as relaxed, receptive, and open as possible. This is what STOP techniques are designed for. Problems with LOOK indicate that you probably need to return and do some more work on step one.

Practice STOP techniques for several days and then assess whether your mind is agitated, restless, confused—all impediments to relaxation. If you see an improvement, begin to add on different LOOK techniques and see how this goes. Keep in mind that downshifting has no negative connotations: It does not mean you've failed, or are hopeless, or need remedial help. This is all simply a part of deepening and perfecting your STOP, LOOK, and LISTEN practice.

Remember, too, that the Downshifting Operating Instruction (page 50) applies anytime and wherever you are in STOP, LOOK, and LISTEN. This means that you can always go back to the preceding step, do an 8-minute session, and then return to the problem step. This is true even after months of practice. Which is why it's called a "practice."

Spaced-Out Versus Spacious Mind

In this LOOK technique, you compare the diametrically opposed states of mind I call "Spaced-Out" and "Spacious."

They may sound similar, but they are light-years apart. Spaced-Out Mind is a product of The Panel; Spacious Mind is the embodiment of The Promise.

We all spend a good deal of our lives in Spaced-Out Mind. Its characteristics include a variety of body sensations and feelings, such as feeling ungrounded, confused, nervous, disoriented, and unable to make decisions. I call this "ADD Lite"—a disease of epidemic proportions, not just in America, but worldwide.

Spaced-Out Mind is the default position of Elsewhere and Elsewhen. It renders you unable to act in the moment because you are too busy weighing past results against future implications. The resultant confusion prevents you from really being able to LOOK at what is happening; this, as we know, leads directly back down the primrose path to The Panel.

The antidote and polar opposite of Spaced-Out Mind is Spacious Mind, a roomy expanse where you can calmly attend to what's coming up with clarity and focus, beyond the restriction of The Panel's mind chatter. This is the domain of Your Best Self—a place of clarity and infinite possibility.

1. Sit in a comfortable position that allows your chest and abdomen to move freely. Sit alertly but not rigidly. Set your timer for 8 minutes.

2. Gently allow your eyes to close. Rest your attention at your chest and abdominal area. Notice your inhale. Notice your exhale. Do this for a few breaths. Relax.

3. Think of an issue in your life that you are trying to resolve. Don't choose a major one. Choose something simple, like what color to paint the kitchen. Observe the impact this issue has on your mind and body. Does it trigger feelings of agitation, fear, anger, frustration? What kinds of thoughts are contained in your "package"?

4. Bring your attention to these thoughts. What are the qualities of the voices that imbue the thoughts you're hearing? Clear, calm, comforting, or supportive? Or fearful, accusative, self-defeating, and negative? If they are the latter, welcome to Spaced-Out Mind, Courtesy of The Panel.

5. Take a deep breath and slowly sigh it out. Do this again. Relax. Return your attention to your issue, and see if you can contact a spacious open vista,

beyond Spaced-Out Mind, a place where thoughts seem to have room to breathe. This is the expanse of Spacious Mind, home base of Your Best Self.

6. Relax into Spacious Mind. There is no need to think about your problem. Allow Spacious Mind to take over, in its own way and its own time. Release your need to control thinking and simply enjoy the ride. Whenever you find yourself plunged back into Spaced-Out Mind, simply realize this and gently return attention to Spacious Mind. Do this until your timer sounds.

How do you feel? Can you see, feel, perhaps even taste, the difference between the quality of your thinking in Spaced-Out Mind versus Spacious Mind? Did you receive a possible solution to your life issue? Was it something "you" might never have thought of? Could it have been there all the time, only you were too spaced-out to notice it?

TROUBLESHOOTING

My mind is overrun with thoughts. There's
no spaciousness.

Your challenge is understandable and common. The following parable might help illuminate the situation:

A Zen student was at his wit's end trying to control his mind. He came before his Zen master, bowed deeply, and implored her to help him overcome his nonstop thinking and become enlightened. Instead of offering instruction, the master clapped her hands for tea. A teapot and two small cups were brought.

The master raised the teapot and began pouring tea into the student's cup, which filled almost instantly. The master continued pouring as tea cascaded over the lip, splashing to the floor.

The student watched in utter surprise and shock. Then, mustering his courage, he said, "Master, you are spilling the tea!" The master smiled and replied, "This teacup is like your mind. There is no room for enlightenment until you discard what already fills it."

Consider the "tea" in your teacup. Is it fresh-brewed daily by The Panel? Probably. What could happen if you emptied your cup? There would be a lot more space in it! How can you do this? By continuing to practice STOP, LOOK, and LISTEN. Allow this process to empty your cup of spaced-out thoughts, and be receptive to spacious ones.

I had a major insight doing Spacious Mind. Can I stop, jot it down, and then go back to practice?

It's best not to stop in the middle of your practice. If your insight is the real deal, chances are good it will be there after you finish your practice session. In fact, your belief you've had a huge insight and must stop everything and jot it down is just another version of The Panel at work, seeking to distract you from where your best interests lie.

My advice is to carry on with your practice until your timer sounds, no matter what comes up. You don't need to write down thoughts or revelations; they're not going to vanish. They've always been there, contained within The Promise of Your Best Self.

7

Step Three: LISTEN

Where You Are

Welcome to the third and final step of STOP, LOOK, and LISTEN.

As you now realize, the words "STOP" and "LOOK" go beyond common definitions, serving as pointers to direct experience. It's the same with LISTEN—perhaps more so. The quality of LISTENing is the most mysterious, indefinable—and powerful—step of STOP, LOOK, and LISTEN. Nonetheless, I'll try to give you as clear a picture of it as I possibly can.

Where You're Going

Just as LOOK has nothing to do with sight, LISTEN has nothing to do with hearing.

Once again, our table:

STOP	Relax	Slow the mind
LOOK	Inquire	Defog the mind
LISTEN	Attune to Your Best Self	Open the mind

LISTEN is about attuning to Your Best Self. And what are the qualities of this attunement?

- allowing whatever comes up to come up
- giving up control to a Spacious Mind that contains everything—*even The Panel*
- trusting your innate wisdom to give you the answers you need

The best—and perhaps only—way to understand LISTEN, as I have told you before, is through direct experience. And the best way for you to do this is through techniques.

LISTEN Techniques

Changing Stations

This technique provides you with a nonverbal understanding of LISTEN. You're going to learn about and compare two radio station frequencies, WPNL for The Panel and WYBS for Your Best Self.

Station WPNL

Imagine a radio tuner with a preset feature that automatically locks on to your favorite station when you switch on the radio. This favorite station's format is all talk, all the time. It's called WPNL, shorthand for—you guessed it— The Panel.

WPNL's programming is predictable: a nonstop harangue/pep talk from different "hosts" calculated to make you want to

acquire goods
get things done

be critical, unkind, and self-punishing

keep occupied every minute of your waking life

WPNL's format is repetitious, banal, boring, and almost guaranteed to render you anxious, unhappy, depressed, hopeless, and fatigued. So why do you listen? Because WPNL is also familiar, comfortable, and predictable, a surefire way to keep you in line and as far away from Your Best Self as The Panel can get you. This means that The Panel will do whatever it takes to keep you from turning the dial to the most exciting, self-empowering, and authentic station on the air: WYBS—Your Best Self.

Station WYBS

WYBS is a superstation. If WPNL broadcasts at 1200 megahertz, WYBS broadcasts at 120,000. You'll never hear negative, self-limiting, or hopeless voices on WYBS. What you will "hear" are

fresh insights

authentic wisdom

encouragement to be Your Best Self

feelings of peace and contentment

WYBS is always broadcasting. The reason you're not receiving it—yet—is that your dial is preset to WPNL. Isn't it time to switch the channel to more positive and empowering fare? You're about to do just that.

1. Sit in a comfortable position that allows your chest and abdomen to move freely. Sit alertly but not rigidly. Set your timer for 8 minutes.

2. Gently allow your eyes to close. Bring your attention to your chest and abdominal area. Notice your inhale. Notice your exhale. Do this for a few breaths.

3. Visualize a radio tuner display. It can be an old-fashioned dial, digital readout, anything you like.

4. Notice self-limiting and negative thoughts that arise. Imagine that they are being broadcast from station WPNL. For the next minute or so, simply "receive" WPNL, listening to its nonstop broadcast of self-limiting and negative thinking.

5. Can you feel the emotional and physical toll of this programming? Does it feel painful, exhausting, or confusing? Does it make you frustrated, angry, even rageful? What could it be like to change stations?

6. Return your attention to your tuning dial. Take a breath and relax into your exhale. Do one round of "Sipping" Breath STOP technique (page 59). Allow your thinking to decelerate. When you notice this happening, do a miniversion of the Live or Memorex technique (page 78). LOOK at The Panel–generated beliefs, concepts, and judgments and observe how they want to distract you.

7. Now start to notice something that might have been there all along: a new, infinitely stronger signal. Allow your attention—in other words, your radio tuner—to naturally and effortlessly home in on this signal. You're tuning in to WYBS.

8. Once you lock in on WYBS, there's nothing else you need do. Simply settle back and LISTEN. At first, this new programming may feel strange, nothing like what you've been hearing on WPNL. That's fine. Allow LISTENing to occur and *attune* to WYBS. Stay like this for a few minutes.

9. Now see if you can trace WYBS's signal back to its source. Don't make a huge effort. Simply attune to the signal, relax, and allow it to carry you back to its origin. Remain tuned to WYBS until your timer sounds.

How did WYBS feel compared to WPNL? Did you recognize a difference in the quality of "programming"? Which station was more familiar? Which one was easier to listen to? More inviting? More helpful and positive? There's no need to formulate answers to these questions; Simply consider them.

TROUBLESHOOTING

I like WYBS. How do I stay tuned?

That's great! Your natural preference for WYBS is a sure sign that you're developing a positive preference for Your Best Self. As for your question, my answer is the same as the great pianist Arthur Rubinstein's, when asked by a passing tourist who did not recognize him, "How do I get to Carnegie Hall?" Rubinstein's answer was, "Practice, practice, practice."

The continuous practice of STOP, LOOK, and LISTEN encourages your internal tuning dial to lock on to—and stay at—WYBS. This natural gravitation to WYBS can develop to the point where you won't even realize you're listening to it. But in the beginning, you have to help things along. As you continue to develop a preference for WYBS, you will find yourself staying there a lot longer. And enjoying every moment.

The LISTENing Room

This next technique will increase your ability to truly LISTEN, as opposed to receiving your information about the world filtered through The Panel. Here's what I mean.

When you listen to something familiar, say, a favorite song, The Panel simultaneously produces a companion sound track of thoughts, memories, and associations. Like whom you were dancing with or dating or in love with when you first heard the song, or where you were when you heard it. These Memorex thoughts in turn create and produce feelings, emotions, and other thoughts. It's your basic hall of mirrors. And it has *nothing* to do with reality.

The Panel's sound tracks don't apply just to "oldies." The sound of a passing car can trigger a sound track like this: "Car . . . hey, I need an oil change . . . should I go to the dealer or mechanic down the street . . . who is more expensive?" Thus, whether you're listening to music or hearing a car, what you're *really listening to is The Panel*! In legal terms, this is called hearsay evidence and is never admissible, because it's unreliable and secondhand. The same is true in your life: When you're not LISTENing, you're leading a "hearsay life" in Elsewhere and Elsewhen, far removed from Your Best Self.

Are you ready to change this? This next technique will help you do just that.

1. Sit comfortably and alert. Set your timer for 8 minutes.

2. Gently allow your eyes to close. Bring your attention to your chest and abdominal area. Notice your inhale. Notice your exhale. Do this for a few breaths.

3. Bring your attention to the area just outside your ears and listen to the external sounds that come to you. Don't discriminate. Allow them all. We'll call them "bare" sounds.

4. When you realize that you are not listening to a sound but *interpreting* it, simply STOP. At this moment, you're listening to The Panel's version of the sound. Take a deep breath. Relax and return your attention to your ear area. And bare sounds. Do this for a few minutes.

5. Now imagine yourself seated in a special LISTENing Room. Visualize the entrance door with a big red sign on it that reads: PANEL ENTRY PROHIBITED.

6. Allow yourself to relax in your LISTENing Room. Allow sounds to come to you and know that The Panel cannot come in. If it does manage to sneak in, don't be upset. Simply regard The Panel the same as you would a rude person talking in the next row at the movies. Annoying, but if you pay attention to what's on-screen, you don't hear him. Do that now. Remain in the LISTENing Room until your timer sounds.

How did it feel just to LISTEN to sound, uncontaminated by the voices of The Panel? Clearer? More vibrant? Richer? Can you see how sounds can be "bare"? Can you take another 8 minutes today and spend it in your LISTENing Room? What would your favorite music sound like here?. Try it!

TROUBLESHOOTING

LISTEN feels scary.

Anxiety, fear, and groundlessness can arise when you first attune to The Promise of Your Best Self. Why is this? How can accepting your birthright feel so wrong?

The answer, as usual, involves The Panel. Each time you

practice STOP, LOOK, and LISTEN, you directly challenge the hardwired beliefs, thoughts, and patterns it has labored so hard to create and distract you with. As you rediscover, accept, and attune to Your Best Self, The Panel naturally pulls out all the stops to ensure that it survives. One of the more effective strategies it has in its arsenal is *fear*.

What can you do? Tell The Panel what the hero always tells the villain in a Western: "Pardner, this town ain't big enough for the both of us."

It's time for you to ride The Panel out of town, and before sunup. STOP, LOOK, and LISTEN techniques provide great ammo to

- STOP anxiety, confusion, and fear with relaxation and thought-deceleration techniques
- LOOK through and beyond the fog of fearful, self-limiting, and unhelpful thoughts with inquiry techniques
- LISTEN and reclaim Your Best Self with attunement techniques

And remember, you are not alone: You've always got the top gunslinger in town standing right beside you: Your Best Self.

"You're Soaking in It"

You might remember a series of Palmolive dishwashing liquid TV spots featuring character actress Nancy Walker in her memorable role of Madge the manicurist. Here's how these commercials usually went:

> Open on Madge holding the wrist of her offscreen client, whose fingers are immersed in a bowl of green soaking liquid. This customer must have just been *kvetching* to Madge about the harshness of her own dish detergent, because Madge is urging her to try "mild Palmolive detergent." In response to the client's question as to whether Palmolive is harsh, Madge chuckles, indicates the client's hand, and says, "You're soaking in it."

In this technique you're also going to "soak in it," but it won't be Palmolive. It will be Your Best Self.

1. Sit in a comfortable position that allows your chest and abdomen to move freely. Sit alertly but not rigidly. Set your timer for 8 minutes.
2. Gently allow your eyes to close. Bring your attention to your chest and abdominal area. Notice your

inhale. Notice your exhale. Do this for a few breaths. Release control of your breathing. Allow your lungs, diaphragm, and chest to expand and contract naturally.

3. Imagine yourself floating in a warm pool, nestled in the locale of your dreams: a beautiful deck at a Japanese spa, the mountains of New Mexico, a perch over the turquoise Aegean Sea. It's your choice. Make the image vivid and luxurious.

4. Languidly soak in your pool. There's nothing you need to do, nowhere to go, nothing to think about. Let go of everything. Then let go of trying to let go.

5. When you are yanked out of your pool by voices of The Panel, just acknowledge this. There's no need for anger, analysis, or putting yourself down. Don't ever get involved. Simply return your attention to soaking in your pool, feeling the sensations of warmth and safety.

6. Now, bring your attention to the boundary between your body and the pool. Relax and release into this boundary. Imagine it dissolve and melt as you relax more and more. And as you do, let go of the idea of a "you" soaking in "a pool" but rather that "just soaking" is happening.

7. Just soak until your timer sounds. And linger as long as you want to.

How do you feel? Was it difficult to release your boundary? Was it easier once you released control of holding on to this "you"? Did the sensation of "just soaking" feel familiar? Where might you have encountered it before? Perhaps in the Changing Stations LISTEN technique? What would it be like to "soak" in this, Your Best Self, while going about your day? Sitting in traffic? At work? Are you willing to immerse yourself in this, Your Best Self? What have you got to lose? Other than The Panel?

TROUBLESHOOTING

I don't get what do you mean by "soaking" in Your Best Self.

You're always soaking in Your Best Self. Remember, The Promise has already been kept. Your Best Self is right here, right now—always. All you need do is to call off the search for it—and simply allow things just to be as they are. Here's an analogy that might help:

You're probably familiar with optical illusions where,

if you gaze at an image long enough, it suddenly transforms into something else. A classic version is the Greek vase that morphs into the profiles of two women facing each other. Then there are the Magic Eye books that present a two-dimensional drawing beneath which lies a three-dimensional object.

How do you get to see the 3-D picture? You can't *make it* appear; you have to *allow* it to appear. You do this by completely relaxing your gaze, not focusing on anything. In other words, you trust that the 3-D picture is there and wait patiently to receive it. When you do, the two-dimensional image suddenly disappears, revealing the 3-D figure beneath.

Think of Your Best Self as that 3-D image. The more you intensely hunt for it or demand that it appear, the more it eludes you. But give up control, and *voilà!* It pops right up! Because it's always been right there.

So relax. Let go of everything—even of the *idea* of letting go of everything.

The Ship Has Sailed

Who hasn't arrived at a crowded, rowdy party—the kind of shindig Yogi Berra described as "so crowded that nobody goes there anymore"—and wanted to leave immediately?

Living with The Panel is like being at one of these bashes, only more so: 24/7, 365. Wouldn't it be great if you could split from this party whenever you wanted to? That's what this next LISTEN technique is about:

1. Sit in a comfortable position that allows your chest and abdomen to move freely. Sit alertly but not rigidly. Set your timer for 8 minutes.

2. Gently allow your eyes to close. Bring your attention to your chest and abdominal area. Notice your inhale. Notice your exhale. Do this for a few breaths.

3. Imagine yourself on the deck of a swanky yacht docked at a wooden pier. Around you, a wild high-octane party rages in full swing. Voices prattle, music blasts—a cacophony of babble, music, and high-pitched laughter. These party people are opinionated, noisy, and intrusive—just like The Panel. Wait a second . . . they *are* The Panel!

4. You're jammed against the railing of the boat, crammed in so tight you can hardly breathe or think. Your only thought is, "How do I get off this yacht?" Relax. Help is on the way.

5. Inhale deeply. Allow your exhale to be slow and natural. Do it again. On this second exhale, see yourself suddenly standing on the dock alongside the yacht, watching the hoopla. It's the same whoops and hollers, eardrum-shattering music, shrill laughter, only now you're mercifully on the outside looking in, simply observing the madness.

6. Suddenly, you hear the yacht's powerful engine rumble to life. A few seconds later, it begins to slowly glide out to sea. At first, the movement is imperceptible, but then the yacht picks up speed. You take this in from dockside and watch the yacht as it moves out into the marina channel, the party on deck still in full swing.

7. Keep your attention on the disappearing yacht. Notice that the din fades as it glides farther out. Maintain your awareness as the yacht grows smaller and the voices trail off. As you do this, you may begin to notice the presence of something else that's been present the whole time but, up until now, drowned out by the cacophony: a vast, silent spaciousness that seems to include everything— the yacht, its revelers, the channel, even the ocean

and sky. Even you. This spaciousness may seem familiar. But don't try to name it. In fact, don't do anything with or about it. Just notice it.

8. There is no need to grasp, manipulate, or do anything with or about this spaciousness. Relax and allow yourself to drop into it. Rest here. Notice any familiarity in this space. When have you felt like this before? Listening to WYBS? "Soaking in it"? Relax and stay connected to this spaciousness until your timer sounds.

How did it feel to be outside the party, removed from the chaos? More peaceful? If The Panel were on that deck what would it feel like to wave, shout "Bon Voyage!" and let it sail away? Is there a better party going on that you haven't noticed? Taking place in that spaciousness? Hosted by Your Best Self?

There is. And you've got an open invitation to attend it anytime you feel like it.

Flavor Enhancer

This technique is a trip down memory lane, designed to show you that you've always been Your Best Self.

1. Sit comfortably and allow your chest and abdomen to move freely and easily. Sit alertly but not rigidly. Set your timer for 8 minutes.

2. Gently allow your eyes to close. Bring your attention to your chest and abdominal area. Simply allow yourself to breathe for a minute or so.

3. Imagine yourself at age five doing something you loved to do. This could be anything from playing a sport to serving tea to your dolls to watching your favorite TV show.

4. As you observe yourself at play, get in touch with the state of "presence" you bring to this activity. It's a state I call "relaxed absorption." If Dad called you to dinner, you probably wouldn't hear him. Rest your attention and soak in relaxed absorption. See if you detect the presence of The Panel. Don't be surprised if you don't: There's no room for it in this, Your Best Self.

5. Now, in a relaxed way, fast-forward to present day. Recall an activity you've done in the last twenty-four hours, like helping your child with math, having lunch with your big client, or coaching softball.

6. Imagine yourself in this activity and get in touch with the quality of your engagement. Were you

completely present? Or on automatic pilot? Were you in a state of relaxed absorption? Or removed, disconnected, and bored? Get a sense of where you were.

7. Now, imagine that you are watching your adult activity and your childhood activity together on a split-screen video. Objectively compare them to each other by posing these questions:

> Where am I in Elsewhere and Elsewhen?
> Where am I present?
> Who is doing this activity? My Best Self? Or The Panel?
> Where do I feel more like "me"?

8. Rest your attention on your dual experiences. When The Panel intrudes and pulls you away, simply realize this and return to where you were. Do this until your timer sounds.

Did you feel the disparity in quality of your two experiences? They are both yours. What accounts for the difference? Perhaps your adult experience was governed by The Panel, while your childhood memory was infused by

Your Best Self. Can you see how wonderful it is to live in Your Best Self? Consider what prevents you from living that way right now, no matter what age you are. Could STOP, LOOK, and LISTEN help you attune to it?

TROUBLESHOOTING

I'm trying to LISTEN, but I think it's too hard.

You're buying into one of The Panel's ploys. How do I know? Because you say, "*I think* it's too hard."

Helplessness, confusion, and feeling overwhelmed are just some of the feelings The Panel will try to instill in you to keep your eyes from the prize: Your Best Self. It's time, as the British say, to "Drive on!" STOP and LOOK at the truth of what The Panel is telling you. Ask yourself if it's true. Trust your own direct experience. Then LISTEN and attune to Your Best Self. Make this new habit your default position in life.

Remember: The Promise has already been kept. The treasure that is your birthright, Your Best Self, awaits you every moment—no matter *what* The Panel says.

8

The Promise in Daily Life

Daily life is where The Panel does aits best to challenge you. What better training ground to practice and perfect STOP, LOOK, and LISTEN, and connect to Your Best Self?

This chapter contains two techniques you can incorporate into your daily life to help you do this. They should be easy and feel familiar.

Your trajectory is upward, but be prepared for speed bumps, glitches, and dead ends along the way. Remember, too, that Your Best Self can never be taken away. It's the embodiment of The Promise—and your birthright.

Rehearsal

This simple technique is very handy when The Panel attempts to upset you about an important upcoming appointment, task, or event.

1. Sit in a comfortable position that allows your chest and abdomen to move freely. Sit alertly but not rigidly.
2. Allow your eyes to close gently. Bring your attention to your chest and abdominal area. Notice your inhale. Notice your exhale. Do this for several breaths.
3. Imagine a recent time when you practiced STOP, LOOK, and LISTEN. Allow yourself to drop into the feelings that took you beyond The Panel's grasp, when you were in attunement with Your Best Self. Stay with these feelings. Soak in them. If The Panel attempts to intrude, go to the LISTENing Room, with the PANEL ENTRY PROHIBITED sign that bars The Panel from entering.

4. When you feel attuned to Your Best Self, visualize your upcoming event. Now, remember the Hot Spots/Cool Spots technique, where you took a cool spot and transferred its qualities to a hot spot (page 66). Do this technique with any self-limiting and negative thoughts you are experiencing in connection with your event. When you have done so, relax and take a deep breath. Then open your eyes.

How do you feel? More confident in your ability to handle not only this event but any event? Do you feel more "yourself" or, more accurately, more Your Best Self? Was the technique simple? Were you able to remember and do Hot Spots/Cool Spots? Good.

STOP, LOOK, and LISTEN techniques are a tool kit to counteract anything The Panel throws at you. Create the habit of using them, whenever you find yourself challenged by old, self-limiting thinking and concepts. Mix and match them to your heart's content. And do whatever feels right.

In The Zone

In this technique, you create a "Safety Zone" to shield you from The Panel's constant onslaught of self-limiting and negative thinking. Another name for this zone? Your Best Self.

1. Sit alertly but not rigidly. Gently allow your eyes to close. Bring your attention to your chest and abdominal area. Notice your inhale. Notice your exhale. Do this for two more breaths.

2. Imagine that you are standing at the curb at a busy traffic intersection. The light is red. If you lower your gaze, you see the familiar parallel white lines delineating the crosswalk. This is your Safety Zone. The traffic on either side represents those negative, frightening, and paralyzing thoughts generated by The Panel.

3. Direct your gaze to the Safety Zone lines as they extend across to the opposite side of the street. Follow them, down the next block, across the next street, through your neighborhood, your town, your state. Imagine these Safety Zone lines extending on to the horizon.

4. Now watch these Safety Zone lines begin to reach upward, higher . . . higher . . . above small buildings, above skyscrapers, up and away into infinity. As they rise, they leave behind two transparent, curtainlike, invulnerable shields.

5. Feel yourself enveloped in this Safety Zone that extends up and out into infinity. Stay here a minute or so and let go of everything. This is how it feels to be Your Best Self.

6. The light turns green and it's safe to cross the street. Step off the curb and start across the intersection. There's no need to be afraid or worried; your Safety Zone envelops you on all sides. When thoughts from The Panel arise and threaten, watch them bounce off the towering walls of your protective shield.

7. Feel how secure and protected you are in the Safety Zone. Realize that this is your true home, Your Best Self, always there awaiting you. Imagine what it would be like to live like this when you are driving, shopping, playing sports, even taking out the trash. It can be this way for you when you STOP, LOOK, and LISTEN.

Remembering Your Best Self

During the Cold War, America built the Distant Early Warning (DEW) system, a string of radar installations that extended across Alaska and Canada. Why? To give us the earliest possible warning if we were under nuclear attack.

The Cold War is over and DEW is obsolete. Still, it provides a paradigm for what I call the STOP, LOOK, and LISTEN Early Warning System. It's a way for you to detect and deflect verbal and emotional attack missiles launched by The Panel. Here's a personal experience to show you what I mean. I think you'll find it familiar.

It's Saturday. I've waited patiently on a long supermarket checkout line. But finally I'm next. I'm about to put my groceries on the conveyor belt when a clerk appears at the checkout register next to mine, looks over, and announces, "I can help the next person."

That's me! I pick up my basket and I'm on my way. But in the two seconds it takes me to get there, a guy has appeared out of nowhere on her line. He's now ahead of me—with twenty items! Of course, this makes me furious. The Panel kicks in, and before I know what's happening, I look at the guy and say, "I was here before you."

He looks at me and then proceeds to ignore me. Now I'm on the verge of going ballistic!

It's then that I notice how shallow my breathing has become, how my entire body is coiled tighter than a rattlesnake. A big ball of "red" has appeared in the center of my chest, and it's growing larger. It is at this moment when I suddenly realize that *I don't like the way I'm feeling*. In other words, my STOP, LOOK, and LISTEN warning alarm has gone off.

What do I do next? Simple: STOP, LOOK, and LISTEN. Here's how this looks in the scenario I've described:

1. Realizing that I am upset, angry, and about to say or do something that makes me feel bad triggers my STOP, LOOK, and LISTEN alarm.
2. I take a deep breath and RELAX until I begin to feel myself "come back to earth."
3. Now that I'm calmer and relaxed, I can see more clearly. I'm ready to LOOK at what really happened, as opposed to what The Panel *tells me* is happening. And I realize that I've been a victim of WYSIWYG: The guy who cut me off had no idea that he had done so. I might also do a miniversion of The Trial to see if allowing him

ahead of me means I'm "guilty" of being weak or having bad karma. The judgment? Not guilty, of course.

4. Now that I realize what has really happened, I'm available to LISTEN, and attune to My Best Self. I now respond *authentically* to what is happening. I might apologize; I might not. But in any event, I have my life back. And I definitely feel better.

Notice that the STOP, LOOK, and LISTEN sequence I described occurred *on a deep, nonverbal level* and automatically. I didn't think, "Oh, I'm angry. I'll stop" or "Now, I'll calm down and listen." This is because I've practiced STOP, LOOK, and LISTEN to the point that the three steps automatically activate. At least most of the time.

I'm not perfect at STOP, LOOK, and LISTEN, and I don't know anyone else who is. I've "lost it" countless times, waiting on lines, in doctors' waiting rooms, on gridlocked freeways, you name it. But I've also made progress. How do I know? *Because I catch myself sooner.* And you will, too, as you continue to make STOP, LOOK, and LISTEN your lifelong habit.

Reconnecting with Your Best Self ·

I've said that Your Best Self is your birthright, the embodiment of The Promise. It is always present, right here,
right now, patiently awaiting you. But just because this is
true doesn't mean you can expect to attune to Your Best
Self 100 percent of the time—not if The Panel has anything to say about it!

So what do you do when you realize that The Panel
has once again taken the upper hand and got you thinking, "Dammit, I was attuned, and now I never will be
again!"

Here's a simple technique that can reconnect you to
Your Best Self—even when you feel it's impossible:

1. Close your eyes and sit comfortably. Take a few
   breaths. Relax and STOP. Really feel your body sitting on your chair, upright and relaxed.
2. State your doubt: "I'll never connect to My Best
   Self."
3. LOOK at your belief. Is it true? Or is it just another
   invitation from The Panel to ruminate, analyze,
   and judge yourself?

4. Now, just LISTEN. Allow yourself to naturally gravitate and attune to WYBS.

5. When you're ready, gently open your eyes.

Were you able, even for an instant, to disregard The Panel's attempt to keep you from tuning in to Your Best Self? What happened when you did? Did you attune to Your Best Self? Was it right there, where you last left it, waiting for you?

In Closing

We've come to the end of the book, but not the end of The Promise. It has been and will always be there for you, ready to reveal the limitless, true treasure that is your birthright: Your Best Self.

I said at the beginning that my goal was to empower you to activate and apply your own innate power to move beyond the self-limiting and negative litany of The Panel. If I have helped you to do this in any way, I'm glad.

But really, you did the work. And you did it because there's something inside you that wants to reclaim what you know beyond any doubt is there: your treasure chest containing a priceless gift.

You.

It's not how long you've forgotten, but how soon you remember. Attune to Your Best Self. And be happy.

Resources

This section lists teachers, books, and materials that can help you in your exploration of The Promise and STOP, LOOK, and LISTEN.

I'm quite selective about whom and what I recommend. I've used all these materials and found them helpful to me. They come from respected authorities, some of whom I know, who present down-to-earth, honest, and insightful ways that have helped me. I believe they can do the same for you.

A Finger Pointing at the Moon

There's a Zen saying that any attempt to describe Zen is merely "a finger pointing at the moon—not the moon." It's the same when it comes to The Promise of Your Best Self. I've said throughout *The Promise* that your primary source of insight stems from *direct experience*. As far as I'm concerned, no CD or book—including this one—can do more than point to the truth of who you truly are.

That said, good books and CDs can play a role at two junctures in your STOP, LOOK, and LISTEN practice:

When you feel stuck. Sometimes The Panel latches on to you like a terrier on your pants leg, and you feel anxious, hopeless, and self-doubting. At times like this, an encouraging chapter from a book or CD can set you back on the road and in the right direction. These "pointing words" can sometimes feel magical, appearing at exactly the right moment for you.

When you feel "separate." Another place where a good resource comes in handy is when you feel as if you're *the only person in the world* who's up against The Panel, or that *your* Panel is the worst one on the planet! At times like these, listening to the voice of a good teacher, especially in the presence of a live audience, can remind you that no human being is immune to The Panel's tactics and ploys. This fact can make you feel less alone with your particular challenges and help defuse The Panel.

STOP

These materials can augment the breathing, meditation, and movement techniques you practiced in STOP.

Breathing

Scott Shaw, *The Little Book of Yoga Breathing* (Weiser Books, 2004).
In the space of only eighty-seven pages, Scott Shaw imparts more than a dozen simple and powerful breathing techniques for everything from chilling out to waking up. Scott's instruction is simple, clear, and powerful.

Ken Cohen, *The Beginner's Guide to Healthy Breathing* audio CD (Sounds True, 2006), www.soundstrue.com.
Ken Cohen's CD is a resource that cuts to the chase. As the liner notes say, "When we feel the pace of life is getting too quick, the pace of the breath also becomes too quick. We need to check in and slow the breath down—to remember to *stop, look, and listen,* and breathe." Sound familiar?

Meditation

Victor Davich, *The Best Guide to Meditation* (Renaissance Books, 1998) *and 8 Minute Meditation: Quiet Your Mind. Change Your Life* (Perigee Books, 2004), www.8minutes .org.

Meditation is one of the foundation skills of STOP, LOOK, and LISTEN. And I'm the author of two popular books on the subject.

The Best Guide to Meditation is a 350-page compendium of everything you ever wanted to know about meditation. It includes discussions of all aspects of meditation, including the basics, the variety of mediation traditions, and instruction in more than fifty different meditation techniques.

8 Minute Meditation is at the opposite end of the spectrum. In only 186 pages, this book tells you everything you need to know about meditation and provides a structured program to help you establish the positive habit of meditation. Your time commitment is only 8 minutes per day, the time between two TV commercials. Its ease and short time frame is one reason why *Time* magazine call *8 Minute Meditation* "the most American form of meditation yet."

If you like the way *The Promise* does things, and if STOP, LOOK, and LISTEN works for you, you'll like *8 Minute Meditation*.

***8 Minute Meditation Guided CD*, http://cdbaby.com/cd/ vdavich.**

The *8 Minute Meditation Guided CD* is not a "book on tape." It's the companion to my book in which I guide you in the 8-minute meditation techniques. With the CD, you simply locate your current *8 Minute Meditation* technique, push Play, and close your eyes. The CD does the rest.

The CD makes *8 Minute Meditation* convenient and even easier. You can download the CD onto your MP3 player and meditate anytime you want. Try it out for free at http://cdbaby.com. It is also available on iTunes and other online music Web sites.

Shinzen Young, www.shinzen.org.

I studied meditation with Shinzen for more than fifteen years and find him one of the most insightful, innovative, and accessible meditation teachers in America. His background includes advanced studies in Eastern philosophy, ordination in Japan as a Buddhist monk, senior translator for a legendary Zen master, and professor of Asian philosophy at Chapman University.

One of the great things about Shinzen is his commitment to provide meditation instruction to everyone, via CDs and the Internet. Many of these offerings are available from Sounds True (www.soundstrue.com) as well as his Web site. I highly recommend his *The Beginner's Guide to Meditation* CD and *Break Through Pain* book, which includes a powerful guided meditation CD featuring Shinzen.

Shinzen's Web site is a first-rate resource to meditation, where you'll find a book's worth of free content. In 2008, he instituted "phoné retreats," which provide the opportunity to interact with him and receive meditation instruction— from the comfort of your own home. You can find out about and sign up for phone retreats at his Basic Mindfulness Web site, www.basicmindfulness.org.

Pema Chödrön, *When Things Fall Apart: Heart Advice for Difficult Times* (Shambhala Publications, 2000).

Pema Chodron is the resident teacher at Gampo Abbey, Nova Scotia, and teaches in the Tibetan Buddhist tradition. Her approach to meditation is clear, supportive, and humorous and her talks and meditation instruction are impeccable. Over the years, Pema has written several popular books, including my favorite, *Start Where You Are* (Shambhala Publications, 2004).

I highly recommend Pema's CD sets, *From Fear to Fearlessness*, *True Happiness,* and *Bodhisattva Mind.* They epitomize the kind of material I've mentioned as most helpful: the encouraging voice of a true teacher with a live audience. You can find these materials at the Sounds True Web site, www.soundstrue.com.

Yoga

Julie Carmen, *Yoga for Hormones,* www.juliecarmen yoga.com.

Julie's classes at Exhale Center for Sacred Movement in Venice, California, are always fresh, inspiring, and engaging. Her yoga CD is the next best thing to doing Downward Facing Dog in her class. The yoga asanas (postures) that Julie will instruct you in can help regulate your weight, improve digestion, and reduce stress. And for you guys out there—don't be put off by the word "hormones": We've got them, too.

Mindful Movement

Thich Nhat Hanh, *Thich Nhat Hanh's Mindful Movements* DVD (Sounds True, 2007), www.soundstrue.com.

Thich Nhat Hanh is a Zen master, scholar, poet, and Nobel Peace Prize nominee. He has taught meditation for decades and published many books and CDs. Two of my favorites are *Peace Is Every Step: The Path of Mindfulness in Everyday Life* (Bantam, 1992) and *The Miracle of Mindfulness* (Beacon Press, 1999). His *Mindful Movements* DVD presents a series of simple, gentle, and relaxing exercises that can help you STOP.

Michael J. Gelb, *Body Learning: An Introduction to the Alexander Technique* (Owl Books, 1996).

The Alexander Technique can increase your awareness of the conditioned way you move your body. Through postural retraining, Alexander teachers can help you correct lifelong patterns that can be causing you both physical and emotional distress.

Michael Gelb's book is a good primer on the Alexander Technique. But to learn and benefit from the Alexander Technique you need a qualified, certified teacher. My Alexander teacher is Virginia Griffith Frank, P.T. Working with Virginia was a truly eye-opening experience and enhanced my STOP, LOOK, and LISTEN practice.

Virginia is in Los Angeles and you can e-mail her at VGF.PT.AT@earthlink.net. For other certified teachers near you, visit the Web site of the American Society for the Alexander Technique, www.alexandertech.org.

LOOK

These materials are excellent companions for when you need to defog your mind.

Josh Baran, *The Tao of Now: Daily Wisdom from Mystics, Sages, Poets, and Saints* (Hampton Roads Publishing Company, 2008).
I've known Josh for more than twenty years. He's the man who coined a phrase you've seen many times in *The Promise:* "Elsewhere and Elsewhen." *The Tao of Now* is the antidote to it. Josh has assembled an anthology of 365 daily wakeup calls for your mind, each one intended to bring you back to the present moment. Josh's book is like owning an internal GPS that directs you back to who you really are— even if you think you're lost and light-years away from it.

Richard Carlson, *Don't Sweat the Small Stuff . . . and It's All Small Stuff* (Hyperion, 1996).
The *Don't Sweat the Small Stuff* books are short, pithy, profound, and humorous collections dedicated to helping you put your life into perspective. The title says it all. And the fact that they are so successful testifies to their power.

Cognitive Therapy

Jeffrey M. Schwartz, M. D., *Brain Lock: Free Yourself from Obsessive-Compulsive Behavior* **(Harper Perennial, 1997), and Judith S. Beck,** *The Beck Diet Solution: Train Your Brain to Think like a Thin Person* **(Oxmoor House, 2007).**

The Trial technique you tried back on page 82 is based on the process known as cognitive therapy, an approach that enables people to challenge, dispute, and change negative and self-limiting habits of thinking. If you are interested in further exploration of cognitive therapy, I recommend these two books, which are written by doctors who are authorities in their respective fields.

Byron Katie, *Loving What Is: Four Questions That Can Change Your Life* **(Three Rivers Press, 2003), www .thework.com.**

Byron Katie is the creator of The Work, a simple, powerful, and effective series of four questions that can help you investigate and challenge even your most obstinate core beliefs. *Loving What Is,* Katie's first book, provides a clear, step-by-step introduction to The Work. It includes transcripts of actual workshops to show you how to use the Four Questions worksheet to inquire into the truth of any core belief.

Katie's Web site contains helpful articles, event listings, and a free download of the worksheet.

Raphael Cushnir, *How Now: 100 Ways to Celebrate the Present Moment* **(Chronicle Books, 2005), www .livingthequestions.org.**

Raphael has presented his simple and wise approach to dealing with life's challenges in *O* magazine and several books, including *Unconditional Bliss: Finding Happiness in the Face of Hardship* (Quest Books, 2000) and *Setting Your Heart on Fire* (Broadway Books, 2003).

How Now presents fun and unexpected ways to be present and LOOK at what is really going on. Raphael gives seminars and workshops throughout the United States and the world. To find more information, free articles, and a list of available books and tapes, visit his Web site.

Anthony de Mello, *Awareness* **(Image, 1990).**

Anthony de Mello was a Jesuit priest who studied in diverse awareness traditions, including Buddhism, Hinduism, and psychology. This book consists of short chapters that contain techniques intended, like STOP, LOOK, and LISTEN, to empower you to go beyond The Panel and attune to Your Best Self.

Darlene Mininni, Ph.D., *The Emotional Toolkit: Seven Power-Skills to Nail Your Bad Feelings* **(St. Martin's Griffin, 2006), www.emotionaltoolkit.com.**

Darlene Mininni has a doctorate in clinical psychology and created UCLA's popular emotional education course. If you like STOP, LOOK, and LISTEN, you'll like *The Emotional Toolkit,* in which Darlene lays out her program of "power-skills" for happiness. She gives frequent lectures and workshops where she teaches these power-skills. For further information about Darlene's book and approach, as well as free materials, including her monthly newsletter, visit her Web site.

LISTEN

Catherine Ingram, *Passionate Presence: Experiencing the Seven Qualities of Awakened Awareness* **(Gotham Books, 2004), www.catherineingram.com.**

Special teachers come from a place of clarity, integrity, and kindness. Catherine Ingram is one of those. She has been one of my teachers, and I have always found her to be humorous, accessible, and compassionate. The words Catherine uses may be different, but they lead to the same place: direct experience of the spaciousness of Your Best Self.

Catherine travels the world, giving public events devoted to the nature of awareness. I have attended a number of them, and they never fail to reward me. Visit her Web site for her schedule, free articles, and CD offerings.

Magic Eye Books, www.magiceye.com.

I mentioned Magic Eye books in the LISTEN chapter. As I said, these images provide great opportunities to practice attunement. They're also a heckuva lot of fun!

The Promise Web Site

www.8minutes.org

As you know from your experience with *The Promise*, when you have the right tools, changing your life doesn't mean you need to give up precious hours of your day. That's why I created 8minutes.org, your trusted resource for quick, effective mental fitness workouts like those you've done in *The Promise*.

I personally select every item on the Web site. They are all economical—budget- and time-wise—easy to do, and can change your life. In just minutes a day.

Check out 8minutes.org for life-changing mental fitness tools like *The Promise* and the *8 Minute Meditation* Guided CDs.

Acknowledgments

As they say, "It takes a village. Or at least a zip code." My heartfelt thanks and kudos to Stephanie Tade, the Westside Special Olympics Softball Team, Josh Baran, Nancy and the brothers at Mt. Cavalry, my instructors at Exhale Yoga and Spectrum Fitness, Alyse Diamond, The Buddha, Ann Buck, Turner Classic Movies, the Santa Monica Public Library, Sheila Curry Oakes, Lifeguard Station 29, Camille Beauchamp, Jackson Browne, the speckled yellow koi at the Miramar Hotel, J. S. Bach, the Santa Monica Farmers' Market, Trader Joe's dark chocolate—and dear friends and family.

About Victor Davich

Before his career as a nonfiction author, Victor Davich spent more than two decades as a copywriter, marketing executive, attorney, screenwriter, and producer at major advertising agencies and entertainment studios, including Y&R, Paramount Pictures, and Universal TV.

This is Victor's third book. His *8 Minute Meditation* is a perennial Amazon bestseller and has been featured in *Time* magazine.

Victor forgoes the de rigueur author biography that typically states, "He lives with his wife, two children, and three Labradoodles in Provence." Because he doesn't.

You are invited to contact him at info@8minutes.org or via www.8minutes.org.